# CAMBRIDGE SCHOOL

# *Shakespeare*

# Macbeth

Edited by Rex Gibson

Series Editor: Rex Gibson
Director, Shakespeare and Schools Project

CAMBRIDGE
UNIVERSITY PRESS

PUBLISHED BY THE PRESS SYNDICATE OF THE UNIVERSITY OF CAMBRIDGE
The Pitt Building, Trumpington Street, Cambridge, United Kingdom

CAMBRIDGE UNIVERSITY PRESS
The Edinburgh Building, Cambridge CB2 2RU, UK
40 West 20th Street, New York, NY 10011–4211, USA
477 Williamstown Road, Port Melbourne, VIC 3207, Australia
Ruiz de Alarcón 13, 28014 Madrid, Spain
Dock House, The Waterfront, Cape Town 8001, South Africa

http://www.cambridge.org

First published 1993
Nineteenth printing 2002

Printed in the United Kingdom by The Burlington Press, Foxton, Cambridge CB2 6SW

*A catalogue record for this book is available from the British Library*

*Library of Congress Cataloguing in Publication data applied for*

ISBN 0 521 42621 9 paperback
ISBN 3 12 576230 8 Klett edition

Prepared for publication by Stenton Associates
Designed by Richard Morris, Stonesfield Design
Picture research by Callie Kendall
Illustrations by Jones and Sewell Associates

*Thanks are due to the following for permission to reproduce photographs:*

Cover: Martin Steingräber; 10, 20, 63, 64, 104, 131*t*, Shakespeare Centre Library, Stratford-upon-Avon; 28, 50, 84, 102, 126, 152*t*, Shakespeare Centre Library, Stratford-upon-Avon: Joe Cocks Studio Collection; 37*t*, Garrick Club / E. T. Archive; 37*bl*, © 1955 renewed 1988, Columbia Pictures Industries Inc., all rights reserved/ British Film Institute; 37*br*, Alistair Muir; 46, 76, 110, Angus McBean; 92*l*, 92*r*, 116 Hulton Deutsch Collection; 131*b*, Christian Brachwitz; 132, Morris Newcombe; 134, Shakespeare Centre Library, Stratford-upon-Avon: Joe Cocks Studio Collection; 142 from *Gustave Doré: das graphische Werke*, v. 2, p. 1052/courtesy of the Faculty of Architecture and History of Art Library, University of Cambridge; 148, © 1971 Columbia Pictures Industries Inc., all rights reserved / British Film Institute.

# Contents

# Cambridge School Shakespeare

This edition of *Macbeth* is part of the *Cambridge School Shakespeare* series. Like every other play in the series, it has been specially prepared to help all students in schools and colleges.

This *Macbeth* aims to be different from other editions of the play. It invites you to bring the play to life in your classroom, hall or drama studio through enjoyable activities that will increase your understanding. Actors have created their different interpretations of the play over the centuries. Similarly, you are encouraged to make up your own mind about *Macbeth*, rather than having someone else's interpretation handed down to you.

*Cambridge School Shakespeare* does not offer you a cut-down or simplified version of the play. This is Shakespeare's language, filled with imaginative possibilities. You will find on every left-hand page: a summary of the action, an explanation of unfamiliar words, a choice of activities on Shakespeare's language, characters and stories.

Between each act and in the pages at the end of the play, you will find notes, illustrations and activities. These will help to increase your understanding of the whole play.

There are a large number of activities to give you the widest choice to suit your own particular needs. Please don't think you have to do every one. Choose the activities that will help you most.

This edition will be of value to you whether you are studying for an examination, reading for pleasure, or thinking of putting on the play to entertain others. You can work on the activities on your own or in groups. Many of the activities suggest a particular group size, but don't be afraid to make up larger or smaller groups to suit your own purposes.

Although you are invited to treat *Macbeth* as a play, you don't need special dramatic or theatrical skills to do the activities. By choosing your activities, and by exploring and experimenting, you can make your own interpretations of Shakespeare's language, characters and stories. Whatever you do, remember that Shakespeare wrote his plays to be acted, watched and enjoyed.

Rex Gibson

This edition of *Macbeth* uses the text of the play established by A. R. Braunmuller in *The New Cambridge Shakespeare.*

# List of characters

## The Royal House of Scotland

DUNCAN   King of Scotland
MALCOLM   his elder son
DONALDBAIN   his younger son

## Thanes (noblemen of Scotland)
## their households and supporters

MACBETH   Thane of Glamis
  later Thane of Cawdor
  later King of Scotland
LADY MACBETH
GENTLEWOMAN   her attendant
SEYTON   Macbeth's armour
  bearer
PORTER   at Macbeth's castle
CAPTAIN   wounded in battle
AN OLD MAN
DOCTOR   of physic
FIRST MURDERER
SECOND MURDERER
THIRD MURDERER

BANQUO
FLEANCE   Banquo's son
MACDUFF   Thane of Fife
LADY MACDUFF
SON OF MACDUFF

ROSS
LENNOX
MENTEITH
ANGUS
CAITHNESS
} other
thanes

## The supernatural world

THREE WITCHES  the weird sisters
THREE APPARITIONS

HECATE   Queen of Witchcraft
THREE OTHER WITCHES

## The English

SIWARD  Earl of Northumberland
YOUNG SIWARD   his son
ENGLISH DOCTOR   at the court of King Edward the Confessor

Lords, Soldiers, Attendants, Servants, Messengers

The play is set in Scotland and England

*Three Witches vow to meet Macbeth after the battle. Their familiar spirits call to them. As they leave, they chant ominous words. Duncan hopes for a battle-report from a wounded Captain.*

## 1 Act it! (in groups of three or more)

The best thing to do with the opening scene is to act it out. It doesn't take long to learn the lines. Present it as dramatically as you can. Prepare sound effects – thunder, rain, battle sounds, cats, toads – and anything else you think you'd hear in such a fearful place. Use your imagination on some of the following to create what you feel is the mood of the opening scene.

How do the Witches enter?
How do they move?
Are they old? young? male? female? (In Shakespeare's time they were played by males.)
Do they like each other? hate each other?
How is each Witch different from the others?
How are they dressed? What are they carrying?
Might they be father, mother and child?
What do they do as they speak?

Electrify your audience!

## 2 Familiars (in pairs)

Witches were believed to have familiar spirits: demons who helped with their evil work. These familiars were usually animals or birds. The First Witch's familiar is a grey cat ('Graymalkin'). The Second Witch has a toad ('Paddock') as her familiar. But the Third Witch does not name her familiar – she says only that she'll come at once ('Anon'). Talk together about what creature the Third Witch's familiar might be. Invent a name and the sound it makes.

---

**Graymalkin/Paddock** grey cat/ toad (see **2** above)
**Alarum** trumpet call to battle
**sergeant** a soldier who, at the time, could be the equivalent of a Captain

**fought/'Gainst my captivity** rescued me from capture

# Macbeth

*[handwritten: 5 Acts | Elizebethan/shakesphere.]*

*[handwritten: Audience or their believed in supernatural.]*

## ACT I  SCENE I
## A desolate place

*Thunder and lightning. Enter three WITCHES*

FIRST WITCH When shall we three meet again?
    In thunder, lightning, or in rain?
SECOND WITCH When the hurly-burly's done,
    When the battle's lost, and won.
THIRD WITCH That will be ere the set of sun.
FIRST WITCH Where the place?
SECOND WITCH Upon the heath.
THIRD WITCH There to meet with Macbeth.
FIRST WITCH I come, Graymalkin.
SECOND WITCH Paddock calls.
THIRD WITCH Anon.
ALL Fair is foul, and foul is fair,
    Hover through the fog and filthy air.

10

*[handwritten: effects to grab attenstion.]*

*[handwritten: Setting of the tone in the Play.]*

*[handwritten: Story of macbeth is based on this theme.]*

*Exeunt*

## ACT I  SCENE 2
## King Duncan's camp near Forres

*[handwritten: outside the war field]*

*Alarum within. Enter King DUNCAN, MALCOLM, DONALDBAIN,*
*LENNOX, with attendants, meeting a bleeding CAPTAIN*

DUNCAN What bloody man is that? He can report,
    As seemeth by his plight, of the revolt
    The newest state.
MALCOLM            This is the sergeant
    Who like a good and hardy soldier fought
    'Gainst my captivity. Hail, brave friend;

5

*[handwritten: Greeting]*

*The wounded Captain reports that although the rebel Macdonald had strong forces, Macbeth personally killed him. Facing an assault by fresh Norwegian troops, Macbeth and Banquo fought on undaunted.*

### 1 The Captain's report (in groups of four to six)

The Captain's story (lines 7–42) is action-packed. Every word counts to create vivid pictures of battle ('the broil'). One person reads slowly, a small section at a time, pausing after each short extract. The others mime the action described. For example, the first few sections might be:

'Doubtful it stood' (mime)
'As two spent swimmers' (mime)
'that do cling together/And choke their art' (mime)
'The merciless Macdonald' (mime), and so on.

You'll find that this activity will help you to understand how Shakespeare packs his language with energy and meaning.

### 2 Echoes of war (in pairs)

One partner reads aloud lines 1–44. The other partner echoes every word to do with war, fighting or armies. Afterwards, talk together about how Shakespeare creates atmosphere through his language (it will help you to know that 'kerns and galloglasses' are lightly and heavily armed soldiers respectively).

### 3 What would the wounded Captain write home?

Imagine that you are the wounded Captain. You have had your wounds dressed, and now you write home to tell your family what has happened. Base your account on lines 1–42. Remember: you are now writing home, not speaking to the king, so you will probably use a different style of language.

---

**Fortune** fickle luck
**whore** prostitute
**Valour's minion** bravery's favourite
**nave to th'chaps** navel to the jaws
**trust their heels** run away
**surveying vantage** seeing an opportunity
**furbished** polished, cleaned
**sooth** truth
**memorise another Golgotha** re-enact a slaughter like Christ's crucifixion

Say to the king, the knowledge of the broil

As thou didst leave it.

CAPTAIN                    Doubtful it stood,

As two spent swimmers that do cling together

And choke their art. The merciless Macdonald

Worthy to be a rebel, for to that                                    10

The multiplying villainies of nature

Do swarm upon him – from the Western Isles

Of kerns and galloglasses is supplied,

And Fortune on his damnèd quarrel smiling,

Showed like a rebel's whore. But all's too weak,            15

For brave Macbeth – well he deserves that name –

Disdaining Fortune, with his brandished steel

Which smoked with bloody execution,

Like Valour's minion carved out his passage

Till he faced the slave,                                               20

Which ne'er shook hands, nor bade farewell to him,

Till he unseamed him from the nave to th'chaps

And fixed his head upon our battlements.

DUNCAN O valiant cousin, worthy gentleman.

CAPTAIN As whence the sun 'gins his reflection,           25

Shipwrecking storms and direful thunders,

So from that spring whence comfort seemed to come,

Discomfort swells. Mark, King of Scotland, mark,

No sooner justice had, with valour armed,

Compelled these skipping kerns to trust their heels,       30

But the Norwegian lord, surveying vantage,

With furbished arms and new supplies of men

Began a fresh assault.

DUNCAN Dismayed not this our captains, Macbeth and Banquo?

CAPTAIN Yes, as sparrows, eagles, or the hare, the lion.   35

If I say sooth, I must report they were

As cannons over-charged with double cracks;

So they doubly redoubled strokes upon the foe.

Except they meant to bathe in reeking wounds

Or memorise another Golgotha,                                      40

I cannot tell.

But I am faint, my gashes cry for help.

*Ross tells that Macbeth has triumphed, capturing Cawdor and obtaining ransom and a favourable peace treaty from the King of Norway. Duncan sentences Cawdor to death and confers his title on Macbeth.*

### 1 What's Macbeth like? (in pairs)

Macbeth has not yet appeared, but already he has been much talked of. From your reading of this scene, brainstorm a list of the qualities that you think Macbeth possesses.

### 2 What did Angus see? (in groups of three)

Angus enters but says nothing. Why not give him a chance to add his version? One person reads Duncan, another reads Ross (lines 47–67). Ross pauses after every punctuation mark. The third person, as Angus, adds their own re-telling of Ross's story, explaining each part of it to the king (who might well ask for some additional information).

### 3 Show the image (in small groups)

Look back through Scene 2 and choose two or three images that you particularly enjoy, for example 'two spent swimmers', 'multiplying villainies of nature', 'a rebel's whore', 'as sparrows, eagles', 'another Golgotha'. Prepare a tableau (a still photograph) of each. Hold the frozen moment for thirty seconds. The other groups guess which images you have chosen.

---

**Thane** nobleman of Scotland
**Bellona** (Roman) goddess of war
**lapped in proof** clad in armour
**self-comparisons** similar actions
**Point against point** sword to
 sword

**composition** a peace treaty
**deign** permit
**Saint Colm's Inch** Isle of Incholm
 (see map, page 60)
**bosom interest** heartfelt concerns
**present** immediate

DUNCAN  So well thy words become thee as thy wounds;
　　　　They smack of honour both. Go get him surgeons.

　　　　　　　　　　　　　　　　　[*Exit Captain, attended*]

　　　　　　　*Enter* ROSS *and* ANGUS

　　　　Who comes here?
MALCOLM　　　*urgent*　The worthy Thane of Ross.　　　　　45
LENNOX  What a haste looks through his eyes! So should he look
　　　　That seems to speak things strange.
ROSS　　　　　　　　　　　　　　God save the king.
DUNCAN  Whence cam'st thou, worthy thane?
ROSS　　　　　　　　　　　　　　From Fife, great king,
　　　　Where the Norwegian banners flout the sky
　　　　And fan our people cold.　　　　　　　　　　　50
　　　　Norway himself, with terrible numbers,
　　　　Assisted by that most disloyal traitor,
*whisker*　The Thane of Cawdor, began a dismal conflict,
　　　　Till that Bellona's bridegroom, lapped in proof,
　　　　Confronted him with self-comparisons,　　　　55
*to much*　Point against point, rebellious arm 'gainst arm,
　　　　Curbing his lavish spirit. And to conclude,
　　　　The victory fell on us –
DUNCAN　　　　　Great happiness! –
ROSS　　　　　　　　　　That now Sweno,
　　　　The Norways' king, craves composition.
　　　　Nor would we deign him burial of his men　　　　60
　　　　Till he disbursed at Saint Colm's Inch
　　　　Ten thousand dollars to our general use.
DUNCAN  No more that Thane of Cawdor shall deceive
*Irony*　Our bosom interest. Go pronounce his present death
　　　　And with his former title greet Macbeth.　　　　65
ROSS  I'll see it done.
DUNCAN  What he hath lost, noble Macbeth hath won.

　　　　　　　　　　　　　　　　　　　*Exeunt*

*The three Witches await Macbeth. They plot to torment a sea-captain whose wife has insulted them. A drum signals the approach of Macbeth.*

---

### 1 Speak the language! (in groups of three to six)

The Witches have a style of speaking all their own. To gain the feel of their language, read aloud all they say from lines 1 to 67.

First, take turns to speak it a line at a time. Next, everyone takes a part for a second reading. Experiment with how you read (for example, two or three people might read together as the First Witch, or you might add movements to the rhythm). Then talk together about the way they speak. How many words can you find to describe their style? (A hint: don't be afraid to use a thesaurus to find appropriate words.)

### 2 The master of the *Tiger*

In 1606 (the year in which *Macbeth* was probably written) an English ship called the *Tiger* did in fact limp home after a disaster-struck voyage of 567 days (7 × 9 × 9). Write the ship-captain's account (based on lines 4–24) of his perilous sea journey. Use your imagination just as Shakespeare did. He was more concerned with the dramatic and imaginative possibilities of the stories he heard and read than with their factual exactness (the storm-battered *Tiger* actually sailed to Japan, and Aleppo is sixty miles inland from the Mediterranean coast).

### 3 'Aroint thee, witch'

Line 5 is the only time in the play when the word 'witch' is used by a character. See pages 131 and 166 for information on why the three weird sisters do not have to appear as conventional witches.

---

| | |
|---|---|
| **Aroint thee** clear off | **forbid** cursed |
| **rump-fed ronyon** pampered slut | **sennights** seven nights |
| **quarters** directions | **bark** ship |
| **card** compass | **pilot** guide who steers ships to |
| **penthouse lid** eyelid | harbour |

# ACT 1   SCENE 3
## A heath

Thunder. Enter the three WITCHES

FIRST WITCH Where hast thou been, sister?
SECOND WITCH Killing swine.
THIRD WITCH                          Sister, where thou?
FIRST WITCH A sailor's wife had chestnuts in her lap
    And munched, and munched, and munched. 'Give me',
      quoth I.
    'Aroint thee, witch', the rump-fed ronyon cries.        5
    Her husband's to Aleppo gone, master o'th'Tiger:
    But in a sieve I'll thither sail,
    And like a rat without a tail,
    I'll do, I'll do, and I'll do.
SECOND WITCH I'll give thee a wind.        10
FIRST WITCH Thou'rt kind.
THIRD WITCH And I another.
FIRST WITCH I myself have all the other,
    And the very ports they blow,
    All the quarters that they know        15
    I'th'shipman's card.
    I'll drain him dry as hay:
    Sleep shall neither night nor day
    Hang upon his penthouse lid;
    He shall live a man forbid.        20
    Weary sennights nine times nine,
    Shall he dwindle, peak, and pine.
    Though his bark cannot be lost,
    Yet it shall be tempest-tossed.
    Look what I have.
SECOND WITCH                  Show me, show me.        25
FIRST WITCH Here I have a pilot's thumb,
    Wrecked as homeward he did come.
                *Drum within*
THIRD WITCH A drum, a drum;
    Macbeth doth come.

*The Witches chant a spell to prepare for their meeting with Macbeth. They greet him with the predictions that he will be Thane of Cawdor and King of Scotland. Banquo demands to know his own future.*

'All hail Macbeth, that shalt be king hereafter.' The three Witches greet Macbeth in a 1949 production at Stratford-upon-Avon. Make up three lines, similar in rhythm and style to lines 46–8, to greet a teacher or another student.

## 1 'So foul and fair a day'

Macbeth's first words (line 36) echo the Witches' last lines in Act 1 Scene 1. But why else might he say them? Try to think of several more reasons.

**weird sisters** (in Anglo-Saxon mythology) goddesses of destiny who predicted the future (see page 36)
**Posters** fast travellers
**charm** spell

**aught** anything
**Glamis** (pronounced 'Glahms', that is, one syllable)
**fantastical** imaginary
**noble having** new titles of nobility
**rapt** spellbound

ALL  The weïrd sisters, hand in hand,                          30
      Posters of the sea and land,
      Thus do go, about, about,
      Thrice to thine, and thrice to mine,
      And thrice again, to make up nine.
      Peace, the charm's wound up.                35

        *Enter* MACBETH *and* BANQUO

MACBETH  So foul and fair a day I have not seen.
BANQUO  How far is't called to Forres? What are these,
      So withered and so wild in their attire,
      That look not like th'inhabitants o'th'earth,
      And yet are on't? – Live you, or are you aught         40
      That man may question? You seem to understand me,
      By each at once her choppy finger laying
      Upon her skinny lips; you should be women
      And yet your beards forbid me to interpret
      That you are so.
MACBETH           Speak if you can: what are you?     45
FIRST WITCH  All hail Macbeth, hail to thee, Thane of Glamis.
SECOND WITCH  All hail Macbeth, hail to thee, Thane of Cawdor.
THIRD WITCH  All hail Macbeth, that shalt be king hereafter.
BANQUO  Good sir, why do you start and seem to fear
      Things that do sound so fair? – I'th'name of truth       50
      Are ye fantastical, or that indeed
      Which outwardly ye show? My noble partner
      You greet with present grace and great prediction
      Of noble having and of royal hope
      That he seems rapt withal. To me you speak not.          55
      If you can look into the seeds of time
      And say which grain will grow and which will not,
      Speak then to me, who neither beg nor fear
      Your favours nor your hate.
FIRST WITCH  Hail.                                             60
SECOND WITCH  Hail.
THIRD WITCH  Hail.

*The Witches prophesy that Banquo's descendants will be kings, but he himself will not. Refusing to answer Macbeth's questions, the Witches vanish. Ross brings news of Duncan's delight at Macbeth's victory.*

## 1 More predictions

Write the Witches' predictions (lines 63–5) for Banquo as a modern horoscope.

## 2 Vanishing Witches (in pairs)

Every director of the play has to solve the practical puzzle of the stage direction 'Witches vanish'. How would you convincingly get them off stage, vanishing before the audience's eyes? Work out your suggestions for making the Witches vanish in a production set somewhere in your school or college.

## 3 Three types of language? (in groups of three)

Here's a director of the play giving advice to actors in rehearsal:

'Speak lines 68–76 fast and angrily
Speak lines 77–86 slow and wonderingly
Speak lines 87–98 pompously and grandly.'

Carry out her suggestions several times, changing parts (or sharing out the lines in any way you like). Then talk together about what you think are the appropriate ways in which the lines should be spoken.

## 4 'Strange images of death' (in groups of six)

Ross praises Macbeth. He reports that fighting the Norwegians, Macbeth made 'strange images of death' (line 95). Work out a tableau of one of these strange images. Use some of the wounded Captain's language (from Scene 2) to accompany your image.

---

**get** be father of
**Sinel** Macbeth's father (see
  page 62)
**Stands not . . . belief** is
  unbelievable
**intelligence** knowledge

**corporal** physical
**the insane root** hemlock, henbane,
  or deadly nightshade (when eaten,
  it produces madness)
**Nothing afeard** not afraid
**post with post** many messages

FIRST WITCH Lesser than Macbeth, and greater.

SECOND WITCH Not so happy, yet much happier.

THIRD WITCH Thou shalt get kings, though thou be none.                    65
    So all hail Macbeth and Banquo.

FIRST WITCH Banquo and Macbeth, all hail.

MACBETH Stay, you imperfect speakers. Tell me more.
    By Sinel's death, I know I am Thane of Glamis,
    But how of Cawdor? The Thane of Cawdor lives                    70
    A prosperous gentleman, and to be king
    Stands not within the prospect of belief,
    No more than to be Cawdor. Say from whence
    You owe this strange intelligence, or why
    Upon this blasted heath you stop our way                    75
    With such prophetic greeting? Speak, I charge you.

*Witches vanish*

BANQUO The earth hath bubbles, as the water has,
    And these are of them. Whither are they vanished?

MACBETH Into the air, and what seemed corporal,
    Melted, as breath into the wind. Would they had stayed.                    80

BANQUO Were such things here as we do speak about?
    Or have we eaten on the insane root,
    That takes the reason prisoner?

MACBETH Your children shall be kings.

BANQUO                    You shall be king.

MACBETH And Thane of Cawdor too: went it not so?                    85

BANQUO To th'selfsame tune and words – who's here?

*Enter* ROSS *and* ANGUS

ROSS The king hath happily received, Macbeth,
    The news of thy success, and when he reads
    Thy personal venture in the rebels' sight,
    His wonders and his praises do contend                    90
    Which should be thine or his. Silenced with that,
    In viewing o'er the rest o'th'selfsame day,
    He finds thee in the stout Norwegian ranks,
    Nothing afeard of what thyself didst make,
    Strange images of death. As thick as tale                    95
    Came post with post, and every one did bear
    Thy praises in his kingdom's great defence,
    And poured them down before him.

Macbeth

*Macbeth is amazed to hear that he is to be Thane of Cawdor. Angus explains that the treacherous thane has been sentenced to death. Banquo warns that the Witches' predictions might lead to evil.*

## 1 The Thane of Cawdor

Angus is not quite sure what treachery the Thane of Cawdor has committed. Help him by writing out the official notice of Cawdor's conviction of treason, giving the reasons. Use lines 107–15 for clues.

## 2 'Why do you dress me/In borrowed robes?' (lines 106–7)

There are many references to clothing throughout *Macbeth*. Watch out for them as you read. Think about how they add to the imaginative impact of the play. There's a subtle 'clothes' reference in line 111, where 'line' also means the lining or reinforcement of a cloak.

## 3 The relationship between Macbeth and Banquo (in pairs)

Macbeth and Banquo have just won a great military victory together. They are comrades in arms. How do they relate together on stage before and after the Witches' prophecies? How do they look at each other as Ross and Angus speak? Work out details of how Macbeth and Banquo behave at each sentence on the opposite page. Then decide what Banquo will say to Ross and Angus as he draws them aside for 'a word'.

**earnest** promise
**addition** new title
**heavy judgement** sentence of death
**line** reinforce
**trusted home** believed fully
**enkindle . . . crown** fire your desire to become king

**instruments of darkness** devils (the Witches?)
**Win us . . . consequence** tell us truths about small matters, but lie about great ones
**Cousins** kinsmen

ANGUS                              We are sent
    To give thee from our royal master thanks;
    Only to herald thee into his sight,                              100
    Not pay thee.
ROSS  And for an earnest of a greater honour,
    He bade me, from him, call thee Thane of Cawdor:
    In which addition, hail most worthy thane,
    For it is thine.
BANQUO                  What, can the devil speak true?              105
MACBETH  The Thane of Cawdor lives. Why do you dress me
    In borrowed robes?
ANGUS                              Who was the thane, lives yet,
    But under heavy judgement bears that life
    Which he deserves to lose.
    Whether he was combined with those of Norway,              110
    Or did line the rebel with hidden help
    And vantage, or that with both he laboured
    In his country's wrack, I know not,
    But treasons capital, confessed and proved,
    Have overthrown him.
MACBETH [*Aside*]              Glamis, and Thane of Cawdor:              115
    The greatest is behind. – Thanks for your pains. –
    [*To Banquo*] Do you not hope your children shall be kings,
    When those that gave the Thane of Cawdor to me
    Promised no less to them?
BANQUO                              That trusted home,
    Might yet enkindle you unto the crown,              120
    Besides the Thane of Cawdor. But 'tis strange,
    And oftentimes, to win us to our harm,
    The instruments of darkness tell us truths;
    Win us with honest trifles, to betray's
    In deepest consequence. –              125
    Cousins, a word, I pray you.

*Macbeth weighs the moral implications of the Witches' prediction. He is
horrified at the thought of killing Duncan, but resolves to accept whatever
has to be. He lies to Banquo about his thoughts.*

## 1 Macbeth's private thoughts (in pairs)

Macbeth's aside (lines 126–41) reveals what is really on his mind.

a To discover the seesawing movements of Macbeth's thoughts, link
hands with your partner and gently pull or push as you speak the
lines to each other. Experiment with different movements to find
the rhythm of the language.

b One person reads everything Macbeth says on the opposite page,
pausing at the end of each sentence. The other person echoes
'Hail, King of Scotland' after each sentence. Change over and
experiment with other echoes.

Talk together about how these two exercises can help you to
understand how Macbeth's imagination is at work.

## 2 Thoughts of murder? (in groups of three)

At six points Macbeth uses expressions that could be thoughts of
himself killing Duncan: 'suggestion' (line 133), 'horrid image' (line
134), 'horrible imaginings' (line 137), 'My thought' (line 138),
'surmise' (line 140), 'what is not' (line 141). Prepare a presentation
in which one person speaks lines 129–41 whilst the other two, at the
six appropriate points, show different versions of the murder.

## 3 Clothes again

Banquo's explanation (lines 141–5) of Macbeth's preoccupation
('rapt' = spellbound) uses the imagery of clothes. New titles, like new
clothes, take time to become familiar.

---

**soliciting** promising of pleasure
**Present fears . . . imaginings** real
dangers are less frightening than
what I can imagine
**function/Is smothered in
surmise** action is imprisoned by
imagination

**Time . . . roughest day** what will
be, will be
**things forgotten** (is Macbeth
lying?)
**The interim having weighed it**
after time for thought

MACBETH [*Aside*]                    Two truths are told,
      As happy prologues to the swelling act
      Of the imperial theme. – I thank you, gentlemen. –
      This supernatural soliciting
      Cannot be ill, cannot be good. If ill,                         130
      Why hath it given me earnest of success,
      Commencing in a truth? I am Thane of Cawdor.
      If good, why do I yield to that suggestion,
      Whose horrid image doth unfix my hair
      And make my seated heart knock at my ribs                     135
      Against the use of nature? Present fears
      Are less than horrible imaginings.
      My thought, whose murder yet is but fantastical,
      Shakes so my single state of man that function
      Is smothered in surmise, and nothing is,                      140
      But what is not.
BANQUO                    Look how our partner's rapt.
MACBETH  If chance will have me king, why chance may crown me
      Without my stir.
BANQUO                    New honours come upon him
      Like our strange garments, cleave not to their mould,
      But with the aid of use.
MACBETH                    Come what come may,                        145
      Time and the hour runs through the roughest day.
BANQUO  Worthy Macbeth, we stay upon your leisure.
MACBETH  Give me your favour. My dull brain was wrought
      With things forgotten. Kind gentlemen, your pains
      Are registered where every day I turn                         150
      The leaf to read them. Let us toward the king.
      [*To Banquo*] Think upon what hath chanced and at more
          time,
      The interim having weighed it, let us speak
      Our free hearts each to other.
BANQUO                    Very gladly.
MACBETH  Till then, enough. – Come, friends.                         155
                             *Exeunt*

*Malcolm reports that the Thane of Cawdor died a repentant and dignified death. Duncan reflects that it is impossible to judge anyone by their outward appearance. He warmly welcomes Macbeth.*

---

## 1 A good death? (in groups of six)

The way in which the Thane of Cawdor died was apparently the noblest thing he did in his life: 'Nothing in his life/Became him like the leaving it'. His death is hardly ever shown on stage (but it is shown in the film version directed by Roman Polanski). Prepare a group presentation to show how Cawdor behaved at his execution. One person narrates lines 5–11 as you stage your scene.

## 2 Appearances are deceptive (whole class)

You can't tell what people are like from their looks, muses Duncan ('There's no art/To find the mind's construction in the face'). Do you agree? Organise a class debate on Duncan's lines 11–12. You may find it helpful to collect photographs from newspapers (for example, of convicted criminals) to use as evidence for your views.

## 3 Dramatic irony (in groups of three)

Dramatic irony occurs when the audience knows something that the characters in the play do not. Duncan's line about Cawdor ('He was a gentleman on whom I built/An absolute trust') and Macbeth's immediate entry is an example of dramatic irony. As Duncan speaks of 'absolute trust', the man who is thinking about murdering him enters. Work out how you think Macbeth should enter to increase the sense of dramatic irony (for example, as a war hero? shiftily? hesitantly? swaggering?, and so on).

---

**Flourish** fanfare of trumpets
**in commission** responsible
**Became** dignified
**studied** rehearsed (a theatrical image)
**before** beyond my power to pay you

**recompense** suitable reward
**That the proportion . . . mine** that I could honour you appropriately
**More is thy due . . . pay** you deserve more than anyone can pay

# ACT 1   SCENE 4
## Duncan's palace at Forres

*Flourish. Enter King* DUNCAN, LENNOX, MALCOLM, DONALDBAIN,
*and attendants*

DUNCAN  Is execution done on Cawdor, or not
    Those in commission yet returned?
MALCOLM                    My liege,
    They are not yet come back. But I have spoke
    With one that saw him die, who did report
    That very frankly he confessed his treasons,           5
    Implored your highness' pardon, and set forth
    A deep repentance. Nothing in his life
    Became him like the leaving it. He died
    As one that had been studied in his death,
    To throw away the dearest thing he owed          10
    As 'twere a careless trifle.
DUNCAN                There's no art
    To find the mind's construction in the face.
    He was a gentleman on whom I built
    An absolute trust.

*Enter* MACBETH, BANQUO, ROSS, *and* ANGUS

              O worthiest cousin,
    The sin of my ingratitude even now           15
    Was heavy on me. Thou art so far before,
    That swiftest wing of recompense is slow
    To overtake thee. Would thou hadst less deserved,
    That the proportion both of thanks and payment
    Might have been mine. Only I have left to say,       20
    More is thy due than more than all can pay.
MACBETH  The service and the loyalty I owe,
    In doing it, pays itself. Your highness' part

*Macbeth declares his loyalty to Duncan, who (after promising honours to Macbeth and Banquo) announces that his son, Malcolm, shall succeed to the throne. Macbeth is appalled and broods ominously.*

## 1 Public compliments and private thoughts (in pairs)

Macbeth's six lines to Duncan (lines 22–7) and his six lines to himself (lines 48–53) are strongly contrasted.

**a** Read both speeches aloud, spreading your arms wide at each word with more than one syllable. What do you notice? Then read the second speech again, rapping out each monosyllable with your fist.

**b** Read lines 22–7, and smile and bow deeply every time you speak a word about loyalty or kingship. Then read lines 48–53 and snarl and make a stabbing gesture every time you speak words that suggest Macbeth's evil intentions.

Now suggest different ways of speaking the two speeches.

Malcolm, having been named as the next king, shakes Macbeth's hand, watched by Duncan (left). At what point in the script opposite do you think this moment, invented by the director, occurs? Does it add to the dramatic effect of the scene?

---

**Wanton** unrestrained
**We will establish our estate upon**
 I declare as Scotland's next king
**invest** endow, clothe
**Inverness** Macbeth's castle
**harbinger** messenger (an officer
 who prepared for a king's visit)

**The eye wink at the hand** don't
 see the fatal blow
**commendations** praises or
 recommendations
**peerless** unmatchable

Is to receive our duties, and our duties
Are to your throne and state, children and servants,                    25
Which do but what they should by doing everything
Safe toward your love and honour.

DUNCAN                                    Welcome hither.
I have begun to plant thee and will labour
To make thee full of growing. Noble Banquo,
That hast no less deserved, nor must be known                          30
No less to have done so, let me enfold thee
And hold thee to my heart.

BANQUO                               There if I grow,
The harvest is your own.

DUNCAN                               My plenteous joys,
Wanton in fullness, seek to hide themselves
In drops of sorrow. Sons, kinsmen, thanes,                             35
And you whose places are the nearest, know:
We will establish our estate upon
Our eldest, Malcolm, whom we name hereafter
The Prince of Cumberland, which honour must
Not unaccompanied invest him only,                                     40
But signs of nobleness like stars shall shine
On all deservers. [*To Macbeth*] From hence to Inverness
And bind us further to you.

MACBETH  The rest is labour which is not used for you;
I'll be myself the harbinger and make joyful                           45
The hearing of my wife with your approach.
So humbly take my leave.

DUNCAN                               My worthy Cawdor.

MACBETH  [*Aside*] The Prince of Cumberland: that is a step
On which I must fall down, or else o'erleap,
For in my way it lies. Stars, hide your fires,                         50
Let not light see my black and deep desires,
The eye wink at the hand. Yet let that be,
Which the eye fears when it is done to see.                  *Exit*

DUNCAN  True, worthy Banquo, he is full so valiant,
And in his commendations I am fed;                                     55
It is a banquet to me. Let's after him,
Whose care is gone before to bid us welcome:
It is a peerless kinsman.
                        *Flourish*

                                                *Exeunt*

*Lady Macbeth reads her husband's letter telling of the Witches' prophecy of kingship. She analyses his nature, fearing that he is too decent and squeamish to murder Duncan for the crown.*

## 1 Macbeth's letter

Lines 1–12 may be only part of Macbeth's letter to his wife. What other news did he report? Write the missing parts of the letter, giving details of the battle and his thoughts about Banquo.

## 2 Breakfast with the Macbeths (in pairs)

Lady Macbeth analyses her husband's nature. In lines 15–23 she describes at least eight elements of his character. How has she come to hold this view of him?

Write your own list of the elements of Macbeth's personality, using lines 15–23 as your guide. Then improvise a breakfast-time conversation between the Macbeths (based on your list) in which Lady Macbeth gives actual examples of his behaviour to support her view.

Two points to help you:

a Lines 22–3 are very densely expressed. They mean 'what you fear, you don't wish to do'.
b Lady Macbeth describes her own style of talking in lines 24–5.

## 3 First impressions

This is Lady Macbeth's first appearance. Talk together how you visualise her (age, costume, physical appearance). Compare your impressions with the illustrations on pages 37, 46, 76, 132 and 134.

---

**in the day of success** on the day of victory in battle
**missives** messengers
**the coming on of time** the future
**What thou art promised** king
**catch the nearest way** act without pity

**illness** evil
**holily** fairly
**Hie** hurry
**golden round** crown
**metaphysical** supernatural
**tidings** news

# Act 1   Scene 5
## Macbeth's castle at Inverness

*Enter* LADY MACBETH *alone, with a letter*

LADY MACBETH [*Reads*] 'They met me in the day of success, and
I have learned by the perfectest report they have more in
them than mortal knowledge. When I burned in desire to
question them further, they made themselves air, into which
they vanished. Whiles I stood rapt in the wonder of it, came      5
missives from the king who all-hailed me Thane of Cawdor, by
which title before these weïrd sisters saluted me and referred
me to the coming on of time, with "Hail, king that shalt be."
This have I thought good to deliver thee, my dearest partner of
greatness, that thou mightst not lose the dues of rejoicing by      10
being ignorant of what greatness is promised thee. Lay it to thy
heart and farewell.'
    Glamis thou art, and Cawdor, and shalt be
    What thou art promised; yet do I fear thy nature,
    It is too full o'th'milk of human kindness      15
    To catch the nearest way. Thou wouldst be great,
    Art not without ambition, but without
    The illness should attend it. What thou wouldst highly,
    That wouldst thou holily; wouldst not play false,
    And yet wouldst wrongly win. Thou'dst have, great
        Glamis,      20
    That which cries, 'Thus thou must do' if thou have it;
    And that which rather thou dost fear to do,
    Than wishest should be undone. Hie thee hither,
    That I may pour my spirits in thine ear
    And chastise with the valour of my tongue      25
    All that impedes thee from the golden round,
    Which fate and metaphysical aid doth seem
    To have thee crowned withal.

*Enter* [ATTENDANT]

                  What is your tidings?
ATTENDANT The king comes here tonight.

*The Attendant gives news that Macbeth is approaching. Lady Macbeth calls on evil spirits to assist her murderous plans. She greets Macbeth with thoughts of future greatness.*

### 1 Lady Macbeth's surprise (in small groups)

Talk together about why Lady Macbeth should say line 29: 'Thou'rt mad to say it'. What's on her mind?

### 2 Is it a spell? (in groups of four)

Speak Lady Macbeth's lines 36–52 as a spell, calling on evil spirits for assistance. Share the lines between you and experiment with different ways of saying them: whisper them; hiss them fiercely; speak them as if in a trance. Is she confident or frightened as she speaks, or in some other mood?

Work out the most effective way of delivering the speech. Add background sound effects to increase the dramatic intensity of your presentation. It may help you to know that the raven was considered to be a bird of ill-omen, associated with death; and when she says 'make thick my blood', Lady Macbeth presumably means that this will stop pity reaching her heart.

### 3 How do they speak?

All actors give much thought to how lines 57–8 should be spoken: 'And when goes hence?'/'Tomorrow, as he purposes'. Are they spoken innocently, or with murder in mind? What advice would you give to both actors?

---

**had the speed of** overtook
**tending** attention, accommodation
**unsex me** remove my gentler
  feelings
**compunctious** compassionate
**fell** deadly, savage

**gall** bitter poison
**pall** wrap (as in a funeral pall or
  cloak)
**dunnest** darkest
**all-hail hereafter** future kingship
**in the instant** now

LADY MACBETH                         Thou'rt mad to say it.
 Is not thy master with him? Who, were't so,   30
 Would have informed for preparation.
ATTENDANT  So please you, it is true: our thane is coming.
 One of my fellows had the speed of him;
 Who almost dead for breath, had scarcely more
 Than would make up his message.
LADY MACBETH                         Give him tending,   35
 He brings great news.

            *Exit* [*Attendant*]
     The raven himself is hoarse,
 That croaks the fatal entrance of Duncan
 Under my battlements. Come, you spirits
 That tend on mortal thoughts, unsex me here
 And fill me from the crown to the toe topfull   40
 Of direst cruelty; make thick my blood,
 Stop up th'access and passage to remorse
 That no compunctious visitings of nature
 Shake my fell purpose nor keep peace between
 Th'effect and it. Come to my woman's breasts   45
 And take my milk for gall, you murd'ring ministers,
 Wherever in your sightless substances
 You wait on nature's mischief. Come, thick night,
 And pall thee in the dunnest smoke of hell,
 That my keen knife see not the wound it makes,   50
 Nor heaven peep through the blanket of the dark,
 To cry, 'Hold, hold.'

     *Enter* MACBETH
     Great Glamis, worthy Cawdor,
 Greater than both by the all-hail hereafter,
 Thy letters have transported me beyond
 This ignorant present, and I feel now   55
 The future in the instant.
MACBETH                         My dearest love,
 Duncan comes here tonight.
LADY MACBETH                         And when goes hence?
MACBETH  Tomorrow, as he purposes.

*Lady Macbeth urges Macbeth to hide his deadly intentions behind welcoming looks. She will manage the killing of Duncan. Banquo and Duncan comment on the benign appearance of Macbeth's castle.*

## 1 Double meanings

Lady Macbeth's lines 64–8 are filled with double meaning: 'provided for' = fed (or killed); 'business' = feasting (or murder); 'dispatch' = carrying out the welcome (or killing). Does Lady Macbeth use these veiled words because she is:

a testing Macbeth: how he will react to the possibility of murder?
b still unsure herself about the awfulness of murder?
c afraid that direct language will make Macbeth refuse to act?

Consider each possibility in turn, then suggest any other probable explanations.

## 2 Can you trust appearances? (in groups of three)

Lines 1–10 are full of praise for the appearance of Macbeth's castle. Duncan admires its position ('seat') and healthy air. Banquo develops an elaborate metaphor as he describes nests of house martins ('loved mansionry') under every convenient ledge ('jutty, frieze, Buttress, . . . coign of vantage'). He voices the belief that martins choose healthy situations to raise their young ('pendent bed', 'procreant cradle'). But in Shakespeare's *The Merchant of Venice*, 'martlet' (or martin) was also used about a visitor who was deceived by appearances ('martin' was a slang term for 'dope' or 'dupe').

Talk together about how you would stage the opening ten lines of Scene 6 so that the audience can see and hear both the benign and malign implications of the words. Remember: they've just seen Lady Macbeth planning Duncan's murder with the words 'look like th'innocent flower, / But be the serpent under't' (look friendly, but act treacherously).

---

**beguile** deceive
**look up clear** put on an innocent look
**To alter . . . fear** a guilty face (favour) reveals itself (or fear results in a guilty face)

**Hautboys** oboes
**seat** position, location
**martlet** martin (see 2 above)
**pendent** hanging

LADY MACBETH                              O never
    Shall sun that morrow see.
    Your face, my thane, is as a book where men                          60
    May read strange matters. To beguile the time,
    Look like the time, bear welcome in your eye,
    Your hand, your tongue; look like th'innocent flower,
    But be the serpent under't. He that's coming
    Must be provided for, and you shall put                              65
    This night's great business into my dispatch,
    Which shall to all our nights and days to come
    Give solely sovereign sway and masterdom.
MACBETH We will speak further –
LADY MACBETH                              Only look up clear;
    To alter favour ever is to fear.                                    70
    Leave all the rest to me.

                                       *Exeunt*

# ACT I   SCENE 6
## Outside Macbeth's castle

*Hautboys, and torches. Enter King* DUNCAN, MALCOLM,
DONALDBAIN, BANQUO, LENNOX, MACDUFF, ROSS, ANGUS,
*and attendants*

DUNCAN  This castle hath a pleasant seat; the air
    Nimbly and sweetly recommends itself
    Unto our gentle senses.
BANQUO                              This guest of summer,
    The temple-haunting martlet, does approve
    By his loved mansionry that the heaven's breath                       5
    Smells wooingly here. No jutty, frieze,
    Buttress, nor coign of vantage but this bird
    Hath made his pendent bed and procreant cradle;
    Where they most breed and haunt, I have observed
    The air is delicate.                                                 10

*Lady Macbeth welcomes Duncan with elaborate courtesy. She speaks of loyalty, obedience and gratefulness for past honours.*

---

## 1 Ceremony and sincerity (in pairs)

Duncan and Lady Macbeth exchange many compliments and much flattery. Duncan's lines 11–15 are full of involved thought and elaborate courtesy. He says that love sometimes causes him trouble, but he is grateful for such love. This should teach Lady Macbeth to ask God to reward Duncan for the trouble he is causing her!

Lady Macbeth's flattery, however, hides a sinister purpose. Speak aloud everything she says in lines 15–29. Every time you say something (as Lady Macbeth) that you think is insincere, bare your teeth menacingly, then smile! (or say 'fair is foul').

Experiment with other ways of showing her hypocrisy. It's helpful to remember that here she is taking her own advice to Macbeth: 'look like th'innocent flower, / But be the serpent under't'.

Identify who's who in the photograph, then decide which line you think is being spoken at this moment.

---

**God yield us** God reward us
**single** weak
**contend** balance, weigh
**those of old** past honours
**late dignities** recent honours
**rest your hermits** will pray for you
  constantly

**coursed** chased, hunted
**purveyor** officer riding ahead to
  prepare food
**in count** in trust (or totally)
**make their audit** show their
  accounts (or give to you)

*Enter* LADY [MACBETH]

DUNCAN  See, see, our honoured hostess. – The love
        That follows us sometime is our trouble,
        Which still we thank as love. Herein I teach you
        How you shall bid God yield us for your pains
        And thank us for your trouble.
LADY MACBETH              All our service,      15
        In every point twice done and then done double,
        Were poor and single business to contend
        Against those honours deep and broad wherewith
        Your majesty loads our house. For those of old,
        And the late dignities heaped up to them,      20
        We rest your hermits.
DUNCAN              Where's the Thane of Cawdor?
        We coursed him at the heels and had a purpose
        To be his purveyor, but he rides well,
        And his great love, sharp as his spur, hath holp him
        To his home before us. Fair and noble hostess,      25
        We are your guest tonight.
LADY MACBETH           Your servants ever
        Have theirs, themselves, and what is theirs in count
        To make their audit at your highness' pleasure,
        Still to return your own.
DUNCAN              Give me your hand;
        Conduct me to mine host: we love him highly      30
        And shall continue our graces towards him.
        By your leave, hostess.
                                    *Exeunt*

> *Macbeth struggles with his conscience: killing Duncan will result in vengeance; there are compelling reasons against the murder. Heaven itself will abhor the deed. Only ambition spurs him on.*

## 1 To kill or not to kill? (in small groups)

Alone on stage, Macbeth agonises over killing Duncan. Experiment with ways of speaking his soliloquy to bring out his uneasy feelings as he thinks aloud. For example, you could share the lines between you and whisper them, heads close together, as a tortured conversation. Use the following analysis of the soliloquy to help your explorations:

lines 1–7  if only there were no consequences resulting from the murder, I'd risk it, not worrying about the future

lines 7–25 the arguments against killing Duncan:

        8–12 vengeance: the killer will be killed

        13–14 kinship: you don't kill your relatives

        13–14 loyalty: you don't kill your king

        14–16 hospitality: a host doesn't kill his guest

        16–20 Duncan's good qualities: you don't kill a virtuous king

        20 (and 7) religion: the killer is damned for eternity

        21–5 pity and horror: murder is unnatural to innocent humanity and to Heaven

lines 25–8 ambition is my only motivation to kill.

## 2 Name the deed! (in pairs)

Macbeth rarely speaks directly of killing Duncan. Instead he uses less brutal language (euphemisms): 'it', ''tis', 'assassination', 'his surcease', 'this blow', 'these cases', 'ingredience', 'the deed', 'bear the knife', 'his taking-off', 'horrid deed', 'my intent'. Read the soliloquy, saying 'killing Duncan' instead of each euphemism. Talk together about the difference the substitutions make.

---

**trammel up the consequence** catch (like netting a fish) the result
**surcease** death, killing
**jump the life to come** Heaven's punishment
**inventor** original teacher

**chalice** cup, goblet
**faculties** powers as king
**cherubin** angelic children
**sightless couriers** wind (blind or invisible runners)

# ACT 1  SCENE 7
## Macbeth's castle  Near the Great Hall

*Hautboys. Torches. Enter a butler and many servants with dishes and service over the stage. Then enter* MACBETH

MACBETH  If it were done when 'tis done, then 'twere well
It were done quickly. If th'assassination
Could trammel up the consequence and catch
With his surcease, success, that but this blow
Might be the be-all and the end-all – here,                    5
But here, upon this bank and shoal of time,
We'd jump the life to come. But in these cases,
We still have judgement here that we but teach
Bloody instructions, which being taught, return
To plague th'inventor. This even-handed justice              10
Commends th'ingredience of our poisoned chalice
To our own lips. He's here in double trust:
First, as I am his kinsman and his subject,
Strong both against the deed; then, as his host,
Who should against his murderer shut the door,               15
Not bear the knife myself. Besides, this Duncan
Hath borne his faculties so meek, hath been
So clear in his great office, that his virtues
Will plead like angels, trumpet-tongued against
The deep damnation of his taking-off.                        20
And pity, like a naked newborn babe
Striding the blast, or heaven's cherubin horsed
Upon the sightless couriers of the air,
Shall blow the horrid deed in every eye,
That tears shall drown the wind. I have no spur              25
To prick the sides of my intent, but only
Vaulting ambition which o'erleaps itself
And falls on th'other –

*Enter* LADY [MACBETH]

How now? What news?

*Macbeth says he has decided not to kill Duncan. Lady Macbeth accuses him of cowardice and lack of manliness. She would kill her own child rather than break such a promise.*

### 1 Why doesn't he argue with her? (in pairs)

Macbeth has just been conscience-stricken by powerful reasons for not murdering Duncan, but now the only reason he gives is little more than 'what will people think?'. Talk together about why you think he doesn't at least tell of the argument he's just had with himself.

### 2 A wife taunts her husband (in groups of six to eight)

One person reads Macbeth; all the others are Lady Macbeth. Macbeth sits or stands in the centre; the Lady Macbeths walk or stand around him. Work through lines 28–82, with each Lady Macbeth reading only up to a punctuation mark before handing on. Hurl your words at Macbeth in any manner you think appropriate.

Try this exercise several times, then discuss which sentence or phrase in all Lady Macbeth's lines (lines 35–72) you think has the greatest effect on Macbeth. ('The poor cat i'th'adage' is probably the cat in the proverb who wanted the fish, but was afraid of the water.)

### 3 Fear of being overheard (in small groups)

Both the Macbeths have left the feast they have prepared for Duncan. At any moment someone may come in and overhear their secret conversation.

- How would you advise the actors to behave throughout the scene?
- Improvise a parallel situation in which two people carry on a tense conversation, fearful of being overheard by their guests.

---

**Not cast aside so soon** not throw away my reputation (opinions) so quickly
**so green and pale** like a hangover
**the ornament of life** life's highest achievement (the crown)
**break this enterprise** suggest killing Duncan

**They have made themselves** now is the time and the place to murder Duncan
**fitness** timeliness
**given suck** suckled a child at my breast (see page 130)
**had I so sworn** if I had promised

LADY MACBETH He has almost supped. Why have you left the
      chamber?

MACBETH Hath he asked for me?

LADY MACBETH                Know you not he has?      30

MACBETH We will proceed no further in this business.
      He hath honoured me of late, and I have bought
      Golden opinions from all sorts of people,
      Which would be worn now in their newest gloss,
      Not cast aside so soon.

LADY MACBETH             Was the hope drunk      35
      Wherein you dressed yourself? Hath it slept since?
      And wakes it now to look so green and pale
      At what it did so freely? From this time,
      Such I account thy love. Art thou afeard
      To be the same in thine own act and valour,      40
      As thou art in desire? Wouldst thou have that
      Which thou esteem'st the ornament of life,
      And live a coward in thine own esteem,
      Letting I dare not wait upon I would,
      Like the poor cat i'th'adage?

MACBETH                   Prithee, peace.      45
      I dare do all that may become a man;
      Who dares do more is none.

LADY MACBETH             What beast was't then
      That made you break this enterprise to me?
      When you durst do it, then you were a man.
      And to be more than what you were, you would      50
      Be so much more the man. Nor time, nor place
      Did then adhere, and yet you would make both.
      They have made themselves and that their fitness now
      Does unmake you. I have given suck and know
      How tender 'tis to love the babe that milks me:      55
      I would, while it was smiling in my face,
      Have plucked my nipple from his boneless gums
      And dashed the brains out, had I so sworn
      As you have done to this.

*Lady Macbeth will make the king's bodyguards so drunk that murdering*
*Duncan (and blaming the bodyguards) will be easy. Macbeth applauds her.*
*He says that they should veil their evil designs with pleasant looks.*

### 1 'We fail?' (in pairs)

There are many ways of speaking these two words (incredulously,
resignedly, and so on). Explore, and decide which version you prefer.

### 2 Evil whispers (in pairs)

Whisper lines 59–82 to each other. Then change roles and laugh your
way through the lines. Afterwards, go back to line 28 and work out the
most appropriate ways to speak the two parts.

### 3 False face

'Away, and mock the time with fairest show,
False face must hide what the false heart doth know.'

Once again a major theme of the play is heard: you can't tell what
people are like from outward appearances. Look back over Act 1 and
collect as many examples as you can which make the same point:
appearances cannot be trusted.

### 4 Metaphors

Line 60: 'Screw your courage to the sticking-place' – like a musician
tightening the strings of a violin; or like an archer turning the screw to
adjust the cord of his crossbow to receive the arrow.

Lines 65–7 use an elaborate metaphor from alchemy, a bogus
science. Drunkenness will make the king's attendants forget their
duties because their reason will be befuddled by noxious vapours
('memory . . . Shall be a fume'). 'Receipt' and 'limbeck' were items of
apparatus used by alchemists.

---

**chamberlains** attendants,
  bodyguards
**wassail** drinking toasts ('Cheers!')
**convince** overpower
**drenchèd** drunken
**spongy** drink-sodden

**quell** slaughter, murder
**mettle** spirit
**receive** interpret
**Each corporal agent** every part of
  me
**mock the time** deceive the world

MACBETH                              If we should fail?
LADY MACBETH                                    We fail?
    But screw your courage to the sticking-place,                    60
    And we'll not fail. When Duncan is asleep,
    Whereto the rather shall his day's hard journey
    Soundly invite him, his two chamberlains
    Will I with wine and wassail so convince
    That memory, the warder of the brain,                            65
    Shall be a fume, and the receipt of reason
    A limbeck only. When in swinish sleep
    Their drenchèd natures lies as in a death,
    What cannot you and I perform upon
    Th'unguarded Duncan? What not put upon                           70
    His spongy officers, who shall bear the guilt
    Of our great quell?
MACBETH                        Bring forth men-children only,
    For thy undaunted mettle should compose
    Nothing but males. Will it not be received,
    When we have marked with blood those sleepy two                  75
    Of his own chamber and used their very daggers,
    That they have done't?
LADY MACBETH                    Who dares receive it other,
    As we shall make our griefs and clamour roar
    Upon his death?
MACBETH                        I am settled and bend up
    Each corporal agent to this terrible feat.                       80
    Away, and mock the time with fairest show,
    False face must hide what the false heart doth know.

                                                 *Exeunt*

# Looking back at Act I
*Activities for groups or individuals*

## 1 Seven scenes: seven headlines

Write a newspaper headline for each of the seven scenes in Act I.
Choose your type of newspaper: serious, sensational, and so on.

## 2 Appearances are deceptive

Things are not what they seem in *Macbeth*. The notion that you
cannot trust outward appearances echoes through Act I:

'Fair is foul, and foul is fair'
'nothing is but what is not'
'Look like th'innocent flower,/But be the serpent under't'
'There's no art/To find the mind's construction in the face'
'To beguile the time, look like the time'
'False face must hide what the false heart doth know'

Identify who makes each remark. Work out a way of presenting each
line (for example, mime or drawing) to illustrate the theme of
deception.

## 3 Witches or weird sisters?

Only once in the entire play does someone use the word 'witch' (see
page 8). Macbeth calls them 'weird sisters'. In Anglo-Saxon mythology these were 'goddesses of destiny' who predicted the future.
Find out about other supernatural beings who might be witches (for
example, furies, fates, harpies, gorgons, sirens, trolls, eldritches).

## 4 Can the future be foretold?

Collect horoscopes from magazines and newspapers. Survey your
class to find how many students believe the future can be foretold.
Invent horoscopes for Duncan, Lady Macbeth, Ross, Malcolm. As
you read on, check to see if your predictions are fulfilled.

## 5 What is 'a man'?

The idea of what it is to be 'a man' runs through the play. Make a list
of eight to twelve qualities that you think 'a man' should possess.
Check how many of those qualities you feel Macbeth possesses.

## 6 Presenting Macbeth and Lady Macbeth

There is no 'one right way' to interpret *Macbeth*. Each new production moves beyond Shakespeare's Jacobean world to express the
ideas, feelings and political and social climate of its own particular
time and culture.

a At Drury Lane Theatre in 1762, David Garrick and Mrs Pritchard
   played in eighteenth-century costumes similar to those worn at
   court at the time.
b *Joe Macbeth* is set in Chicago's gangland. It follows Shakespeare's
   play closely, using the conventions of the gangster movie.
c *From a Jack to a King*, a 1992 rock musical adaptation of *Macbeth*.

Talk together about where you would set your production of *Macbeth*,
and how you would present Macbeth and Lady Macbeth.

*Banquo tells of Duncan's gratitude for the Macbeths' hospitality. When Banquo says he has dreamt of the Witches, Macbeth replies with a lie. Banquo won't be tempted by Macbeth into betraying Duncan.*

## 1 Banquo's dream

Banquo hints at the 'cursèd thoughts' that come in sleep (lines 8–9). He tells that he has dreamt of the Witches (line 20). Just what did Banquo dream? Write a story or poem entitled 'Banquo's dream'.

## 2 Contrast Banquo and Macbeth (in groups of three)

Opposite, Shakespeare shows the difference between Banquo, the honourable man, and Macbeth, the deceiver. Banquo conscientiously fights evil thoughts ('Restrain in me'). He uses kind and open words in his report of Duncan. He wishes to stay free of guilt ('keep/My bosom franchised') and remain loyal ('allegiance clear') to Duncan (lines 26–9).

In sharp contrast, Macbeth speaks untruths: 'A friend'; 'Being unprepared'; 'I think not of them'. He tries to tempt Banquo to his side ('cleave to my consent') in return for honour (lines 25–6).

Prepare advice to the actors in order to alert the audience to the contrast between the two men. To help you prepare read lines 10–30, but with two people reading Macbeth (one as Macbeth, one as his evil conscience). At the end of each line Macbeth speaks, the 'evil conscience' says 'False face must hide what the false heart doth know'.

## 3 Fleance questions his father (in pairs)

Imagine that as Fleance and Banquo walk away (after line 30), Fleance asks his father, 'What was all that about?'. Improvise the conversation that follows.

---

**husbandry** thrift, in putting out the candles (stars)
**powers** angels who protect against evil
**largess to your offices** gifts to your servants' quarters

**shut up** gone to bed
**Being unprepared . . . wrought** the fact that Duncan's visit was unexpected meant we didn't entertain him as fully as we would have wished

# ACT 2   SCENE 1
## Macbeth's castle   The courtyard

*Enter* BANQUO, *and* FLEANCE *with a torch-bearer before him*

BANQUO  How goes the night, boy?
FLEANCE  The moon is down; I have not heard the clock.
BANQUO  And she goes down at twelve.
FLEANCE                              I take't, 'tis later, sir.
BANQUO  Hold, take my sword. – There's husbandry in heaven,
    Their candles are all out. – Take thee that too.    5
    A heavy summons lies like lead upon me,
    And yet I would not sleep; merciful powers,
    Restrain in me the cursèd thoughts that nature
    Gives way to in repose.
        *Enter* MACBETH, *and a Servant with a torch*
            Give me my sword –
    Who's there?    10
MACBETH  A friend.
BANQUO  What, sir, not yet at rest? The king's abed.
    He hath been in unusual pleasure
    And sent forth great largess to your offices.
    This diamond he greets your wife withal,    15
    By the name of most kind hostess, and shut up
    In measureless content.
MACBETH                      Being unprepared,
    Our will became the servant to defect,
    Which else should free have wrought.
BANQUO                                    All's well.
    I dreamed last night of the three weïrd sisters;    20
    To you they have showed some truth.
MACBETH                                I think not of them;
    Yet when we can entreat an hour to serve,
    We would spend it in some words upon that business,
    If you would grant the time.
BANQUO                          At your kind'st leisure.
MACBETH  If you shall cleave to my consent, when 'tis,    25
    It shall make honour for you.
BANQUO                            So I lose none
    In seeking to augment it, but still keep
    My bosom franchised and allegiance clear,
    I shall be counselled.

*Alone, Macbeth hallucinates, thinking he sees a blood-stained dagger. As he moves to murder Duncan, his thoughts are filled with evil images.*

---

### 1 Does the audience see the dagger? (whole class)

Half the class argues for a dagger to be shown on stage (for example, as a laser image). The other half argues against. Take a vote at the end.

### 2 Act out Macbeth's thoughts (in pairs or small groups)

One person reads the soliloquy, a sentence or short section at a time. The others act out what Macbeth does or describes. Add sound effects if necessary (for example, how can you make the bell dramatically significant?).

### 3 Images of evil (in groups of six or more)

Lines 49–56 show Macbeth's imaginings of evil at work. Make a presentation in any form you think appropriate (for example, a mime, a series of tableaux) to show each image: nature, wicked dreams, witchcraft, murder, Tarquin. Notice that 'murder' is a personification (imagined as a person).

### 4 Bring on the Witches (in groups of four)

Act out Macbeth's lines 33–64 with the Witches taking a leading part in the action. Work out what they might do at every section of Macbeth's soliloquy.

Afterwards, talk together about how convincing it would be to use the Witches to stage-manage affairs throughout Macbeth's soliloquy.

---

**sensible/To feeling** able to be touched
**heat-oppressèd** feverish
**palpable** real, physical
**dudgeon** handle
**gouts** large drops

**Hecate** goddess of witchcraft
**off'rings** gifts, sacrifices
**Tarquin** Roman prince who raped Lucrece
**prate** talk
**knell** funeral bell

MACBETH                    Good repose the while.

BANQUO  Thanks, sir; the like to you.                                30

                *[Exeunt] Banquo[, Fleance, and Torch-bearer]*

MACBETH  *[To Servant]* Go bid thy mistress, when my drink is
          ready,
      She strike upon the bell. Get thee to bed.

                                                *Exit [Servant]*

Is this a dagger which I see before me,
The handle toward my hand? Come, let me clutch thee:
I have thee not, and yet I see thee still.                           35
Art thou not, fatal vision, sensible
To feeling as to sight? Or art thou but
A dagger of the mind, a false creation,
Proceeding from the heat-oppressèd brain?
I see thee yet, in form as palpable                                  40
As this which now I draw.
Thou marshall'st me the way that I was going,
And such an instrument I was to use.
Mine eyes are made the fools o'th'other senses,
Or else worth all the rest. I see thee still                         45
And on thy blade and dudgeon gouts of blood,
Which was not so before. There's no such thing:
It is the bloody business which informs
Thus to mine eyes. Now o'er the one half-world
Nature seems dead, and wicked dreams abuse                           50
The curtained sleep. Witchcraft celebrates
Pale Hecate's off'rings, and withered murder,
Alarumed by his sentinel, the wolf,
Whose howl's his watch, thus with his stealthy pace,
With Tarquin's ravishing strides, towards his design                55
Moves like a ghost. Thou sure and firm-set earth,
Hear not my steps, which way they walk, for fear
Thy very stones prate of my whereabout,
And take the present horror from the time,
Which now suits with it. Whiles I threat, he lives;                 60
Words to the heat of deeds too cold breath gives.
                          *A bell rings*
I go, and it is done. The bell invites me.
Hear it not, Duncan, for it is a knell
That summons thee to heaven or to hell.              *Exit*

*Lady Macbeth, exhilarated by drink, awaits Macbeth's return from Duncan's room. She has drugged Duncan's bodyguards, but fears that the murder has not been done. Macbeth returns and says he has killed the king.*

## 1  After the murder (in pairs)

Take parts as Lady Macbeth and Macbeth. Read straight through the whole scene. (Don't pause to worry over words you are not sure of.) Then exchange roles and read through again.

- Talk together about the atmosphere of the scene and your impressions of the characters. Who is the dominant partner?
- What should be the pace of playing different sections of the scene? Work out a set of notes advising the actors where they should speak quickly, and where they should adopt a different style of speech. Give reasons for your advice.

## 2  Nervousness? (in pairs)

Explore different ways of staging lines 13–24 ('My husband? . . . sorry sight'). Remember: it's a dark night, Macbeth has just committed a terrible killing, and the Macbeths are hosts to the murdered king and his family.

## 3  A different view of Lady Macbeth?

Something stops Lady Macbeth from killing Duncan herself: 'Had he not resembled / My father as he slept, I had done't' (Lines 12–13). Choose one of the following as a title, and write a short story or poem:

- The childhood of Lady Macbeth: as told by herself
- The childhood of Lady Macbeth: as told by her father
- Lady Macbeth and the sleeping Duncan.

---

**quenched** silenced, drugged
**fatal bellman** watchman who rang the bell before executions and burials
**surfeited grooms** drunken servants

**mock their charge** abandon their duties
**possets** hot drinks
**owl, crickets** (both associated with death)
**chamber** bedroom

42

# ACT 2  SCENE 2
## Macbeth's castle    Near Duncan's room

*Enter* LADY MACBETH

LADY MACBETH  That which hath made them drunk, hath made
    me bold;
What hath quenched them, hath given me fire.
     [*An owl shrieks*]
                         Hark, peace!
It was the owl that shrieked, the fatal bellman
Which gives the stern'st good-night. He is about it.
The doors are open, and the surfeited grooms        5
Do mock their charge with snores. I have drugged their
    possets,
That death and nature do contend about them,
Whether they live, or die.

*Enter* MACBETH [*with two bloody daggers*]

MACBETH                Who's there? What ho?
LADY MACBETH  Alack, I am afraid they have awaked,
    And 'tis not done; th'attempt and not the deed    10
    Confounds us – hark – I laid their daggers ready,
    He could not miss 'em. Had he not resembled
    My father as he slept, I had done't. My husband?
MACBETH  I have done the deed. Didst thou not hear a noise?
LADY MACBETH  I heard the owl scream and the crickets cry.    15
    Did not you speak?
MACBETH  When?
LADY MACBETH  Now.
MACBETH  As I descended?
LADY MACBETH  Ay.                            20
MACBETH  Hark, who lies i'th'second chamber?
LADY MACBETH  Donaldbain.
MACBETH  This is a sorry sight.
LADY MACBETH  A foolish thought, to say a sorry sight.

*Macbeth is obsessed by his inability to say 'Amen', and by a voice crying that he has murdered sleep and will never sleep again. Lady Macbeth dismisses his hallucinations and orders him to return the daggers. He refuses.*

## 1 Conscience strikes (in groups of five or six)

Macbeth is conscience-stricken as he struggles to say 'Amen'. Not being able to speak the word implies that God will not bless him and he is doomed to eternal damnation. Macbeth also thinks that he hears a voice foretelling that he will sleep no more. Some actors portray Macbeth as talking to himself, ignoring his wife. Other actors show him feverishly telling her his story, as if she can offer help. How would you recommend Macbeth should speak lines 24–46? How should Lady Macbeth say line 43: 'What do you mean?'?

## 2 Off stage or on stage? (in pairs)

Shakespeare chose not to show the actual killing of Duncan. If you were directing the play, would you insert a scene showing the murder? Talk together about the possible gains and losses of such a scene.

## 3 Who are the sleepers?

No one can be really sure who the two sleepers are: the two grooms or Donaldbain and Malcolm. Look closely at lines 24–9 and think of two or three reasons to justify your choice of the servants or the king's sons – or some other pair.

## 4 Sleep (in groups of four)

Macbeth lists six or seven qualities of sleep in lines 39–43. Work out a mime to show each quality. You could extend your mime by adding the results of lack of sleep promised by the First Witch in Act 1 Scene 3, lines 18–22.

---

**addressed them/Again** went back
**hangman's hands** blood-covered
  hands (executioners often
  disembowelled condemned men)
**ravelled sleeve** frayed sleeve, or
  tangled silk

**sore labour's bath** hard work's
  cure
**Balm** healing medicine
**second course** main item of a meal
**unbend** relax, weaken
**grooms** servants, bodyguards

MACBETH There's one did laugh in's sleep, and one cried,
   'Murder!',             25
   That they did wake each other; I stood, and heard them,
   But they did say their prayers and addressed them
   Again to sleep.
LADY MACBETH     There are two lodged together.
MACBETH One cried 'God bless us!' and 'Amen' the other,
   As they had seen me with these hangman's hands.   30
   List'ning their fear, I could not say 'Amen'
   When they did say 'God bless us.'
LADY MACBETH Consider it not so deeply.
MACBETH But wherefore could not I pronounce 'Amen'?
   I had most need of blessing and 'Amen'     35
   Stuck in my throat.
LADY MACBETH     These deeds must not be thought
   After these ways; so, it will make us mad.
MACBETH Methought I heard a voice cry, 'Sleep no more:
   Macbeth does murder sleep', the innocent sleep,
   Sleep that knits up the ravelled sleeve of care,   40
   The death of each day's life, sore labour's bath,
   Balm of hurt minds, great nature's second course,
   Chief nourisher in life's feast.
LADY MACBETH       What do you mean?
MACBETH Still it cried, 'Sleep no more' to all the house;
   'Glamis hath murdered sleep', and therefore Cawdor   45
   Shall sleep no more: Macbeth shall sleep no more.
LADY MACBETH Who was it, that thus cried? Why, worthy thane,
   You do unbend your noble strength to think
   So brain-sickly of things. Go get some water
   And wash this filthy witness from your hand.    50
   Why did you bring these daggers from the place?
   They must lie there. Go carry them and smear
   The sleepy grooms with blood.
MACBETH        I'll go no more.
   I am afraid to think what I have done;
   Look on't again, I dare not.

*Lady Macbeth takes the daggers to smear Duncan's blood on his servants' faces. A knocking sound frightens Macbeth, but his wife tells him to pull himself together. She plans an alibi.*

## 1 Two kinds of language

Lines 65 and 66 say the same thing in very different ways: with long words ('Latinate') and with short words ('Anglo-Saxon'). As Macbeth gazes on his blood-stained hands, he is appalled to think what he has done. He feels that not all the water in the ocean can clean away the blood. Rather, his hands will make the measureless seas bloody.

Make up several examples of your own in which you first say something in short simple words, then the same thing in long elaborate words. When might you use one style rather than another?

'Give me the daggers.' How accurately do you think the expressions and postures of the Macbeths embody their feelings at this moment?

---

**gild** paint with blood (a pun on gild/guilt)
**withal** with it (blood)
**Neptune** god of the sea

**incarnadine** make blood-red
**Your constancy . . . unattended** you've lost your nerve

46

LADY MACBETH                  Infirm of purpose!                    55
    Give me the daggers. The sleeping and the dead
    Are but as pictures; 'tis the eye of childhood
    That fears a painted devil. If he do bleed,
    I'll gild the faces of the grooms withal,
    For it must seem their guilt.                    *Exit*
                *Knock within*
MACBETH                  Whence is that knocking?                    60
    How is't with me, when every noise appals me?
    What hands are here? Ha: they pluck out mine eyes.
    Will all great Neptune's ocean wash this blood
    Clean from my hand? No: this my hand will rather
    The multitudinous seas incarnadine,                    65
    Making the green one red.

          *Enter* LADY [MACBETH]

LADY MACBETH My hands are of your colour, but I shame
    To wear a heart so white.
           *Knock [within]*
              I hear a knocking
    At the south entry. Retire we to our chamber;
    A little water clears us of this deed.                    70
    How easy is it then! Your constancy
    Hath left you unattended.
           *Knock [within]*
             Hark, more knocking.
    Get on your night-gown, lest occasion call us
    And show us to be watchers. Be not lost
    So poorly in your thoughts.                    75
MACBETH To know my deed, 'twere best not know myself.
           *Knock [within]*
    Wake Duncan with thy knocking: I would thou couldst.
                     *Exeunt*

*Macbeth's Porter imagines himself keeper of Hell's gate. He talks about admitting to Hell a greedy farmer, a liar and a cheating tailor. He jokes with Macduff about the effects of too much drink.*

### 1 Did Shakespeare write it? (in small groups)

Some productions cut the 'Porter scene' altogether, on the grounds that it is not by Shakespeare. But what do you think? Talk together about the case for and against including the Porter scene. To help you, here are a few of the arguments for inclusion.

*Comic relief?* The audience needs a space for laughter.

*Time to change?* The Macbeths need time to change into nightgowns.

*A link with older plays?* In medieval miracle plays a porter at Hell's mouth admitted sinners to the torments of Hell (everlasting bonfire).

*Giving a job to the comedian?* Shakespeare's company, the King's Men, always included one major actor who specialised in comic parts.

*Contemporary jokes?* The Porter's jokes could be about things that were very familiar to audiences in 1606, when the play was first performed: greedy farmers, equivocators (see page 165), cheating tailors and sexually transmitted disease ('roast your goose').

*A commentary on the themes of the play?* Damnation ('everlasting bonfire'); evil and the supernatural (Beelzebub); ambition (the greedy farmer); lying and deceit (equivocator); theft (the tailor); desire and achievement (the effects of drink). (See page 162.)

*The best test?* The best way of deciding whether to include the scene is to act out lines 1–34. Try it!

### 2 The effects of drink (in pairs)

Invent actions ('business') that the Porter could use to accompany his list of the effects of drink (lines 21–30).

---

**old** plenty of
**Beelzebub** the Devil
**equivocator** someone who juggles
  with the truth (see page 165)
**French hose** baggy trousers
**everlasting bonfire** eternal
  damnation in Hell

**carousing** drinking
**second cock** 3 a.m.
**Marry** by the Virgin Mary
**Equivocates** tricks
**giving him the lie** tricking him

# ACT 2   SCENE 3
## The entrance to Macbeth's castle

*Enter a* PORTER. *Knocking within*

PORTER Here's a knocking indeed: if a man were porter of hell-
gate, he should have old turning the key. (*Knock*) Knock, knock,
knock. Who's there i'th'name of Beelzebub? Here's a farmer
that hanged himself on th'expectation of plenty. Come in time
– have napkins enough about you, here you'll sweat for't.     5
(*Knock*) Knock, knock. Who's there in th'other devil's name?
Faith, here's an equivocator that could swear in both the scales
against either scale, who committed treason enough for God's
sake, yet could not equivocate to heaven. O, come in, equivocator. (*Knock*) Knock, knock, knock. Who's there? Faith,     10
here's an English tailor come hither for stealing out of a French
hose. Come in, tailor, here you may roast your goose. (*Knock*)
Knock, knock. Never at quiet: what are you? But this place is
too cold for hell. I'll devil-porter it no further: I had thought to
have let in some of all professions that go the primrose way     15
to th'everlasting bonfire. (*Knock*) Anon, anon. I pray you,
remember the porter. [*Opens door*]

*Enter* MACDUFF *and* LENNOX

MACDUFF Was it so late, friend, ere you went to bed,
　　That you do lie so late?
PORTER Faith, sir, we were carousing till the second cock, and     20
drink, sir, is a great provoker of three things.
MACDUFF What three things does drink especially provoke?
PORTER Marry, sir, nose-painting, sleep, and urine. Lechery, sir, it
provokes, and unprovokes: it provokes the desire, but it takes
away the performance. Therefore much drink may be said to be     25
an equivocator with lechery: it makes him, and it mars him; it
sets him on, and it takes him off; it persuades him and dis-
heartens him, makes him stand to and not stand to. In con-
clusion, equivocates him in a sleep, and giving him the lie,
leaves him.     30

49

*Macduff has come to meet Duncan. Macbeth shows him to Duncan's room.*
*Lennox tells of the terrible events of the night. Horrified, Macduff*
*returns from Duncan's room.*

'Remember the Porter' (Don't forget to tip me). Some modern stage porters ad-lib jokes about contemporary events; others exploit the sexual references to the full or tell 'knock, knock' jokes. But in nineteenth-century Germany, the Porter was a very sober figure who sang a joyful and innocent song to welcome the sunrise. How would the Porter in your production behave?

## 1 What did Lennox hear? (in groups of four)

Prepare a presentation of lines 46–53 that includes all the sounds Lennox heard. If possible, make an audiotape of your presentation.

## 2 Should the audience laugh?

How should Macbeth say line 53? As a reply to Lennox's fearful story it can have very different effects on the audience!

---

**gave thee the lie** knocked you out
**requited him for his lie** paid him back for his wrestling trick
**cast** throw down, or throw up (vomit)
**timely** early
**The labour . . . pain** the work I enjoy cures pain

**limited** appointed
**dire combustion** terrible fires and explosions (an echo of the Gunpowder Plot?)
**obscure bird** owl (associated with death)

MACDUFF  I believe drink gave thee the lie last night.

PORTER  That it did, sir, i'the very throat on me, but I requited him for his lie, and, I think, being too strong for him, though he took up my legs sometime, yet I made a shift to cast him.

*Enter* MACBETH

MACDUFF  Is thy master stirring?                                        35
    Our knocking has awaked him: here he comes.

                                                        [*Exit Porter*]

LENNOX  Good morrow, noble sir.

MACBETH                              Good morrow, both.

MACDUFF  Is the king stirring, worthy thane?

MACBETH                                Not yet.

MACDUFF  He did command me to call timely on him;
    I have almost slipped the hour.

MACBETH                        I'll bring you to him.             40

MACDUFF  I know this is a joyful trouble to you, but yet 'tis one.

MACBETH  The labour we delight in physics pain. This is the door.

MACDUFF  I'll make so bold to call, for 'tis my limited service.   *Exit*

LENNOX  Goes the king hence today?

MACBETH  He does – he did appoint so.                               45

LENNOX  The night has been unruly: where we lay,
    Our chimneys were blown down, and, as they say,
    Lamentings heard i'th'air, strange screams of death
    And prophesying with accents terrible
    Of dire combustion and confused events,                        50
    New hatched to th'woeful time. The obscure bird
    Clamoured the livelong night. Some say, the earth
    Was feverous and did shake.

MACBETH                      'Twas a rough night.

LENNOX  My young remembrance cannot parallel
    A fellow to it.                                                55

*Enter* MACDUFF

MACDUFF  O horror, horror, horror,
    Tongue nor heart cannot conceive, nor name thee.

MACBETH *and* LENNOX What's the matter?

*Macduff, horror-struck, reveals the murder of Duncan. He tells Macbeth and Lennox to see for themselves. He shouts to awake Banquo and the king's sons. Lady Macbeth and Banquo enter, to be told the news.*

---

## 1 'Confusion now hath made his masterpiece'
(in large groups)

To gain a sense of the terrifying confusion that results from Duncan's murder, try this activity. You will need a large space: the Hall or drama studio will be ideal, but it will work in a cleared classroom.

Everybody reads the whole page opposite, but each person begins at a different line. Start anywhere you wish in lines 59–83. As you walk around the room, greet others with a line or more of the script. They will exchange a different line with you, then move on to greet others. Greet as many people as you can, telling each a different part of your story. Don't worry about which character is speaking, just say all the lines in any order (there are at least twenty-seven 'segments' of the script).

Keep the activity going for several minutes, then meet in groups of four or five. Read through again, taking turns, a short section at a time, as quickly as you can. Afterwards, think about these questions:

**a** Could lines 59–83 be rewritten in a different order (and perhaps given to different speakers) and still be meaningful?

**b** How would you stage the page opposite to greatest dramatic effect?

## 2 'Gentle lady'?

Macduff calls Lady Macbeth 'gentle' and says the news is too cruel for a woman's hearing (lines 76–9). From your knowledge of her so far, write down six or seven adjectives to describe her that you think are more suitable than 'gentle'.

---

**Gorgon** Medusa, a mythical woman with snakes for hair; anyone who saw her was turned to stone

**counterfeit** imitation
**The great doom's image** (see page 63)
**parley** talk with

MACDUFF  Confusion now hath made his masterpiece:
        Most sacrilegious murder hath broke ope                    60
        The Lord's anointed temple and stole thence
        The life o'th'building.
MACBETH  What is't you say, the life?
LENNOX  Mean you his majesty?
MACDUFF  Approach the chamber and destroy your sight              65
        With a new Gorgon. Do not bid me speak:
        See and then speak yourselves.
                        *Exeunt Macbeth and Lennox*
                        Awake, awake!
        Ring the alarum bell! Murder and treason!
        Banquo and Donaldbain! Malcolm, awake,
        Shake off this downy sleep, death's counterfeit,             70
        And look on death itself. Up, up, and see
        The great doom's image. Malcolm, Banquo,
        As from your graves rise up and walk like sprites
        To countenance this horror.

         *Bell rings. Enter* LADY [MACBETH]

LADY MACBETH                What's the business
        That such a hideous trumpet calls to parley                  75
        The sleepers of the house? Speak, speak.
MACDUFF                      O gentle lady,
        'Tis not for you to hear what I can speak.
        The repetition in a woman's ear
        Would murder as it fell. –

         *Enter* BANQUO

                O Banquo, Banquo,
        Our royal master's murdered.
LADY MACBETH              Woe, alas.                          80
        What, in our house?
BANQUO               Too cruel, anywhere.
        Dear Duff, I prithee contradict thyself
        And say it is not so.

*Macbeth says that Duncan's death empties the world of meaning. Duncan's sons are told the news of their father's murder. Macbeth defends his killing of the bodyguards. Lady Macbeth faints and is carried out.*

## 1 Does he sound sincere? (in pairs)

Macbeth's two longer speeches opposite raise interesting questions about how language can hide truth as well as reveal it.

In lines 84–9 Macbeth says that Duncan's death makes trivial ('toys') everything worthwhile in life ('renown and grace'). Duncan was 'The wine of life' and everyone else in the world is far inferior ('the mere lees') – but it was Macbeth himself who killed Duncan.

In lines 101–11 Macbeth elaborately defends his killing of Duncan's attendants. He uses language rich in evocative imagery ('silver', 'golden', 'trade', 'Unmannerly breeched') – but he knows that what he says is false.

Read both speeches to each other several times. Talk together about whether Macbeth sounds sincere or insincere. Look ahead to lines 129–30 to discover if your views match Malcolm's.

## 2 'O, by whom?' (in groups of eight)

Who has done the murder? Only two people on stage know the truth. Take parts and prepare a tableau of line 93 to show just how everyone looks at the moment when Malcolm asks his question. Who is suspicious of whom? Who looks at whom, and who avoids eye-contact? Compare the tableaux of each group, identifying who's who and their suspicions.

## 3 Does she really faint? (in groups of four)

Is Lady Macbeth's swoon genuine or not? Two people argue that it's real, two argue that it's faked.

---

**mortality** human destiny or life
**drawn** finished, empty
**lees** dregs (as in a wine glass)
**vault** world (and a pun on wine vault)
**temp'rate** even-tempered

**Th'expedition** the haste
**the pauser, reason** delaying thought
**Unmannerly breeched** rudely covered
**gore** blood

*Enter* MACBETH *and* LENNOX

MACBETH  Had I but died an hour before this chance,
　　　　I had lived a blessèd time, for from this instant,　　　　85
　　　　There's nothing serious in mortality.
　　　　All is but toys; renown and grace is dead,
　　　　The wine of life is drawn, and the mere lees
　　　　Is left this vault to brag of.

*Enter* MALCOLM *and* DONALDBAIN

DONALDBAIN  What is amiss?
MACBETH　　　　　　　　　You are, and do not know't.　　　90
　　　　The spring, the head, the fountain of your blood
　　　　Is stopped, the very source of it is stopped.
MACDUFF  Your royal father's murdered.
MALCOLM　　　　　　　　　O, by whom?
LENNOX  Those of his chamber, as it seemed, had done't.
　　　　Their hands and faces were all badged with blood,　　　95
　　　　So were their daggers which, unwiped, we found
　　　　Upon their pillows. They stared and were distracted;
　　　　No man's life was to be trusted with them.
MACBETH  O, yet I do repent me of my fury
　　　　That I did kill them.
MACDUFF　　　　　　　　Wherefore did you so?　　　100
MACBETH  Who can be wise, amazed, temp'rate, and furious,
　　　　Loyal and neutral, in a moment? No man.
　　　　Th'expedition of my violent love
　　　　Outran the pauser, reason. Here lay Duncan,
　　　　His silver skin laced with his golden blood　　　105
　　　　And his gashed stabs looked like a breach in nature,
　　　　For ruin's wasteful entrance. There the murderers,
　　　　Steeped in the colours of their trade; their daggers
　　　　Unmannerly breeched with gore. Who could refrain,
　　　　That had a heart to love and in that heart　　　110
　　　　Courage to make's love known?
LADY MACBETH　　　　　　　Help me hence, ho.
MACDUFF  Look to the lady.

　　　　　　　　　　　[*Exit Lady Macbeth, helped*]

55

*Donaldbain and Malcolm fear for their future. Banquo and the others swear to investigate the murder. Duncan's sons, suspecting danger, resolve to flee: Malcolm to England, Donaldbain to Ireland.*

## 1 The investigation (in groups of six to eight)

Banquo proposes a meeting to investigate the murder. Everyone is under suspicion. The meeting is not shown on stage. Carry out your own enquiry. Everyone chooses a character who was in the castle at the time. One by one, each character is questioned by everyone else. Remember: whatever happens, you don't want the guilt fixed on you!

## 2 Banquo and Macbeth: another contrast

What do the declarations of Banquo ('In the great hand of God I stand', line 123) and Macbeth ('put on manly readiness', line 126) suggest to you about the differences in their characters?

## 3 'There's daggers in men's smiles' (in groups of four)

Present line 133 in the most imaginative way you can. Remind yourselves of other lines earlier in the play which express the same idea (see page 36). Find two other lines opposite which express the same idea.

## 4 But are they sensible? (in pairs)

Malcolm and Donaldbain don't wish to join with ('consort') the other thanes. They fear that their kinsmen are likely to murder them: 'the nea'er . . . bloody' (lines 133–4). Stealing away in these circumstances is legitimate 'theft': 'There's warrant . . . left' (lines 138–9). But do you think they take the most sensible decision? Compile as many reasons as you can for and against their decision to flee.

---

**auger hole** tiny hole
**brewed** mature
**upon the foot of motion** ready to express
**naked frailties** unclothed bodies (or weak feelings)

**scruples** doubts
**undivulged pretence** hidden purposes
**consort** join
**an office** a duty
**shaft** arrow

MALCOLM [*To Donaldbain*] Why do we hold our tongues, that most
      may claim
    This argument for ours?
DONALDBAIN [*To Malcolm*]     What should be spoken here,
    Where our fate hid in an auger hole may rush      115
    And seize us? Let's away. Our tears are not yet brewed.
MALCOLM Nor our strong sorrow upon the foot of motion.
BANQUO Look to the lady,
    And when we have our naked frailties hid
    That suffer in exposure, let us meet      120
    And question this most bloody piece of work
    To know it further. Fears and scruples shake us:
    In the great hand of God I stand and thence
    Against the undivulged pretence I fight
    Of treasonous malice.
MACDUFF          And so do I.
ALL             So all.      125
MACBETH Let's briefly put on manly readiness
    And meet i'th'hall together.
ALL          Well contented.
          *Exeunt [all but Malcolm and Donaldbain]*
MALCOLM What will you do? Let's not consort with them.
    To show an unfelt sorrow is an office
    Which the false man does easy. I'll to England.      130
DONALDBAIN To Ireland, I. Our separated fortune
    Shall keep us both the safer. Where we are,
    There's daggers in men's smiles; the nea'er in blood,
    The nearer bloody.
MALCOLM        This murderous shaft that's shot
    Hath not yet lighted, and our safest way      135
    Is to avoid the aim. Therefore to horse,
    And let us not be dainty of leave-taking,
    But shift away. There's warrant in that theft
    Which steals itself when there's no mercy left.
              *Exeunt*

*Ross and an Old Man talk about the darkness and unnaturalness of events that mirror Duncan's murder. The sun is obscured, owls kill falcons, and Duncan's horses eat each other. Macduff arrives.*

### 1 Unnatural acts (in pairs)

Darkness in daytime, owls killing falcons, horses eating each other. These strange and terrible disruptions in nature mirror Macbeth's killing of Duncan. Improvise further conversation between Ross and the Old Man. Invent other unusual events that reflect the consequences of the murder.

### 2 Who is the Old Man?

This is the Old Man's only appearance in the play. His dramatic function is rather like the chorus in a Greek tragedy. There, the chorus comments on the action, shows its universality (how the action is reflected in society and nature), and represents the point of view of the ordinary people.

First, decide whether the Old Man fulfils those three functions as a kind of chorus. Then consider him as a character who has grown old under the rule of the feuding war-lords of Scotland. Write his autobiography, using lines 1–4 ('Hours dreadful and things strange') as your inspiration. You will find additional help on page 164. Remember, he's spent his long life in an embattled military society.

### 3 Ross: can you believe him? (in groups of four)

Ross is a thane, a high-ranking nobleman. Did he really see Duncan's horses eating each other (lines 19–20)? Or are there other explanations for what he says? Suggest one or two possible reasons why he claims to have seen such an improbable sight.

---

**Threescore and ten** seventy years
**Hath trifled former knowings**
  has made past events seem trivial
**heavens/act/stage** (theatrical
  metaphors)

**travelling lamp** sun
**the day's shame** Duncan's murder
**entomb** bury
**minions** favourites, the best
**stalls** stables

# ACT 2 SCENE 4
## Outside Macbeth's castle

*Enter* ROSS, *with an* OLD MAN

OLD MAN  Threescore and ten I can remember well;
        Within the volume of which time, I have seen
        Hours dreadful and things strange, but this sore night
        Hath trifled former knowings.
ROSS                  Ha, good father,
        Thou seest the heavens, as troubled with man's act,      5
        Threatens his bloody stage. By th'clock 'tis day
        And yet dark night strangles the travelling lamp.
        Is't night's predominance, or the day's shame,
        That darkness does the face of earth entomb
        When living light should kiss it?
OLD MAN                'Tis unnatural,     10
        Even like the deed that's done. On Tuesday last,
        A falcon tow'ring in her pride of place
        Was by a mousing owl hawked at and killed.
ROSS  And Duncan's horses, a thing most strange and certain,
        Beauteous and swift, the minions of their race,     15
        Turned wild in nature, broke their stalls, flung out,
        Contending 'gainst obedience as they would
        Make war with mankind.
OLD MAN              'Tis said, they eat each other.
ROSS  They did so, to th'amazement of mine eyes
        That looked upon't.

*Enter* MACDUFF

            Here comes the good Macduff.     20
    How goes the world, sir, now?
MACDUFF              Why, see you not?

*Macduff tells that Duncan's sons bribed the killers and have now fled.*
*Macbeth has been elected king, and has gone to Scone to be crowned.*
*Macduff will not attend the ceremony. The Old Man blesses peacemakers.*

## 1 Macbeth's Scotland

- Make your own map of Scotland and design pictures or emblems to illustrate the various locations.

- Find out all you can about Scone and Iona (Colmkill). In addition to the historical facts you discover, include in your report a section on the symbolic significance of these two places in the play.

'Where the place?' The map shows the three places mentioned opposite, and all the other locations of the play. It also shows the territories of the thanes.

---

**suborned** bribed (to murder Duncan)
**Thriftless** greedy
**ravin up** devour
**named** elected king by the thanes (see page 62)

**Scone** a palace near Perth, where Kings of Scotland were crowned
**Colmkill** Iona, the traditional burial place of Kings of Scotland
**Fife** Macduff's territory
**benison** blessing

ROSS  Is't known who did this more than bloody deed?

MACDUFF  Those that Macbeth hath slain.

ROSS                                              Alas the day,
        What good could they pretend?

MACDUFF                              They were suborned.
        Malcolm and Donaldbain, the king's two sons,                    25
        Are stol'n away and fled, which puts upon them
        Suspicion of the deed.

ROSS                              'Gainst nature still.
        Thriftless ambition that will ravin up
        Thine own life's means. Then 'tis most like
        The sovereignty will fall upon Macbeth.                          30

MACDUFF  He is already named and gone to Scone
        To be invested.

ROSS  Where is Duncan's body?

MACDUFF                          Carried to Colmkill,
        The sacred storehouse of his predecessors
        And guardian of their bones.

ROSS                                      Will you to Scone?              35

MACDUFF  No, cousin, I'll to Fife.

ROSS                          Well, I will thither.

MACDUFF  Well may you see things well done there. Adieu,
        Lest our old robes sit easier than our new.

ROSS  Farewell, father.

OLD MAN  God's benison go with you, and with those                       40
        That would make good of bad, and friends of foes.

                                                        *Exeunt*

# Looking back at Act 2
*Activities for groups or individuals*

## 1 Macbeth's castle

All four scenes in Act 2 are set in or near Macbeth's castle at Inverness. Prepare two drawings. The first shows the plan of the castle, locating where different episodes take place. The second is a sketch of the set the audience sees. It should enable the action of each scene to flow easily into the next.

## 2 What did the servant see and hear?

Imagine that you are one of Macbeth's servants at Inverness. You have watched Macbeth's behaviour since he returned from the wars, and overheard snatches of what he and Lady Macbeth said. Write a letter home to tell what you know.

## 3 The election of Macbeth as king

In the eleventh century, Kings of Scotland were elected by their fellow thanes. The title did not automatically descend from father to son. As the family tree below shows, Macbeth had a strong claim to be king, both in his own right and through his wife (granddaughter of a former high king). What happened at the meeting (not shown by Shakespeare) when Macbeth was 'named' as king? Were there

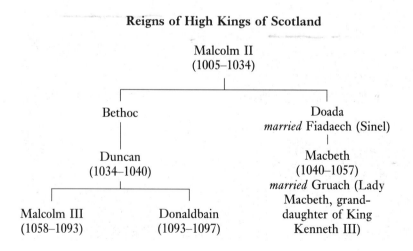

**Reigns of High Kings of Scotland**

Malcolm II
(1005–1034)

Bethoc

Doada
*married* Fiadaech (Sinel)

Duncan
(1034–1040)

Macbeth
(1040–1057)
*married* Gruach (Lady
Macbeth, grand-
daughter of King
Kenneth III)

Malcolm III
(1058–1093)

Donaldbain
(1093–1097)

arguments over his right to succeed? Did anyone speak up for the claims of Malcolm or Donaldbain? Improvise the meeting of the Scottish thanes that resulted in the election of Macbeth.

## 4 Shakespeare's memory?

When Macduff shouts 'Up, up and see / The great doom's image' (Scene 3, line 72), is Shakespeare recalling his schooldays? The vision of the Day of Judgement is painted on the wall of the Guild Chapel in Stratford-upon-Avon, next door to Shakespeare's school. As a schoolboy he must have seen the painting often. Similar wall-paintings (called dooms) were in many churches. They showed all the dead rising from their graves on the Last Day to be judged as to whether they went to Heaven or Hell. If you go to Stratford-upon-Avon, go into the Guild Chapel and look at the doom with lines 71–4 in your mind.

Macbeth

*Banquo fears that Macbeth has become king by evil means, but he takes heart from the Witches' predictions for his own descendants. Macbeth requests Banquo to attend tonight's banquet.*

'Thou hast it now, King, Cawdor, Glamis, all.' Macbeth now wears the crown of Scotland, but does his 'mind's construction' show in his face?

**stand in thy posterity** remain in your family
**verities** truths
**oracles** prophets

**Sennet** trumpet call (of seven notes)
**all thing** totally

# ACT 3    SCENE 1
## The royal palace at Forres

*Enter* BANQUO *dressed for riding*

BANQUO  Thou hast it now, King, Cawdor, Glamis, all,
As the weïrd women promised, and I fear
Thou played'st most foully for't; yet it was said
It should not stand in thy posterity,
But that myself should be the root and father          5
Of many kings. If there come truth from them –
As upon thee, Macbeth, their speeches shine –
Why by the verities on thee made good,
May they not be my oracles as well
And set me up in hope? But hush, no more.          10

*Sennet sounded. Enter* MACBETH *as King,* LADY [MACBETH *as*
*Queen,*] LENNOX, ROSS, *Lords, and Attendants*

MACBETH  Here's our chief guest.
LADY MACBETH                              If he had been forgotten,
It had been as a gap in our great feast
And all thing unbecoming.
MACBETH  Tonight we hold a solemn supper, sir,
And I'll request your presence.
BANQUO                              Let your highness          15
Command upon me, to the which my duties
Are with a most indissoluble tie
Forever knit.

*After checking on Banquo's movements, Macbeth claims that Duncan's sons are spreading malicious rumours. He establishes that Fleance will ride with Banquo, then dismisses the court.*

## 1 Macbeth's real thoughts? (in pairs)

Macbeth has evil intentions for Banquo, but he hides them behind apparently well-meaning words. He also mentions several times that he wants Banquo's advice.

One person reads slowly all Macbeth's words in lines 11–41. The other says 'false face' every time he says something insincere – and adds what is really on his mind!

## 2 'Strange invention' (in groups of three or four)

What was the 'strange invention' (terrible lies) that Macbeth claims Duncan's sons are spreading? Improvise a conversation between Malcolm and some English courtiers as they talk about Macbeth. Does Malcolm speak the truth or lie?

## 3 Why is Lady Macbeth dismissed?

In many productions, Lady Macbeth approaches Macbeth at line 45, obviously wanting to talk, but is dismissed with 'While then, God be with you.'

Why does Macbeth send his wife away with the rest of the court? Imagine that you are a thane who has seen the coronation and attended on Macbeth at court. Write a diary entry that reports on the Macbeths' relationship.

---

**still** always
**grave and prosperous** wise and helpful
**Go not my horse the better** If my horse isn't speedy
**parricide** father's murder

**strange invention** terrible lies, rumours
**Craving us jointly** requiring the attention of both of us
**without** outside

MACBETH  Ride you this afternoon?
BANQUO  Ay, my good lord.                                    20
MACBETH  We should have else desired your good advice
    Which still hath been both grave and prosperous
    In this day's council: but we'll take tomorrow.
    Is't far you ride?
BANQUO  As far, my lord, as will fill up the time            25
    'Twixt this and supper. Go not my horse the better,
    I must become a borrower of the night
    For a dark hour, or twain.
MACBETH  Fail not our feast.
BANQUO  My lord, I will not.                                 30
MACBETH  We hear our bloody cousins are bestowed
    In England and in Ireland, not confessing
    Their cruel parricide, filling their hearers
    With strange invention. But of that tomorrow,
    When therewithal we shall have cause of state           35
    Craving us jointly. Hie you to horse; adieu,
    Till you return at night. Goes Fleance with you?
BANQUO  Ay, my good lord; our time does call upon's.
MACBETH  I wish your horses swift and sure of foot,
    And so I do commend you to their backs.                  40
    Farewell.
                                            *Exit Banquo*
    Let every man be master of his time
    Till seven at night; to make society
    The sweeter welcome, we will keep ourself
    Till supper-time alone. While then, God be with you.     45
                    *Exeunt [all but Macbeth and a Servant]*
    Sirrah, a word with you: attend those men
    Our pleasure?
SERVANT  They are, my lord, without the palace gate.

67

Macbeth

*Macbeth broods on his fears that Banquo's descendants will become kings. The two Murderers enter, and Macbeth reminds them of an earlier conversation when he told them that Banquo is their enemy.*

## 1 Macbeth's secret thoughts (in pairs)

As he waits for the Murderers, Macbeth reveals his most secret thoughts. It's nothing to be king ('thus') unless he is safely king. Banquo is like a thorn in his flesh (just as, in Ancient Rome, Mark Antony was said to be in fear of Octavius Caesar). Try one or both of the following activities on Macbeth's soliloquy (lines 49–73):

a One person reads; the other echoes any word to do with Banquo ('him', 'he', and so on), and any word to do with Macbeth ('I', 'my', 'mine', and so on).

b Take a pencil in your hands. Imagine that it is Banquo. Read the speech, and treat the pencil as if it were Banquo. You may surprise yourself at what you do!

## 2 The Witches' predictions (in small groups)

Both Banquo and Macbeth seem obsessed by the Witches' prophecies. Explore ways of putting together lines 1–10 and lines 58–65 to make a dramatic presentation.

## 3 Yesterday: 'Our last conference' (in groups of three)

Macbeth has had an earlier meeting with the Murderers. He told them ('passed in probation with you') that Banquo has deceived them ('borne in hand'), and it was all Banquo's doing that they were so poor and out of luck ('held you so under fortune'). Improvise that earlier conversation as Macbeth lays all the blame on Banquo. Take lines 77–83 and 85–9 as your starting point.

**thus** king
**dauntless** fearless
**genius** guardian angel
**chid** chided, challenged
**gripe** grasp
**with an unlineal hand** by someone not of my family

**issue** descendants
**filed** defiled
**eternal jewel** soul
**list** jousting tournament, battlefield
**utterance** death
**crossed** double crossed

MACBETH  Bring them before us.   *soliloquy*

*Exit Servant*

To be thus is nothing,
But to be safely thus. Our fears in Banquo          50
Stick deep, and in his royalty of nature
Reigns that which would be feared. 'Tis much he dares,
And to that dauntless temper of his mind,
He hath a wisdom that doth guide his valour
To act in safety. There is none but he,                   55
Whose being I do fear; and under him
My genius is rebuked, as it is said
Mark Antony's was by Caesar. He chid the sisters
When first they put the name of king upon me
And bade them speak to him. Then prophet-like,
They hailed him father to a line of kings.                60
Upon my head they placed a fruitless crown
And put a barren sceptre in my gripe,
Thence to be wrenched with an unlineal hand,
No son of mine succeeding. If't be so,
For Banquo's issue have I filed my mind;                  65
For them, the gracious Duncan have I murdered,
Put rancours in the vessel of my peace
Only for them, and mine eternal jewel
Given to the common enemy of man,
To make them kings, the seeds of Banquo kings.           70
Rather than so, come Fate into the list,
And champion me to th'utterance. Who's there?

*Enter Servant and two* MURDERERS

[*To Servant*] Now go to the door and stay there till we call.

*Exit Servant*

Was it not yesterday we spoke together?                   75
MURDERERS  It was, so please your highness.
MACBETH  Well then, now have you considered of my speeches?
Know, that it was he in the times past which held you so under
fortune, which you thought had been our innocent self. This I
made good to you in our last conference; passed in probation   80
with you how you were borne in hand, how crossed; the instruments, who wrought with them, and all things else that might to
half a soul and to a notion crazed say, 'Thus did Banquo.'

69

*Macbeth taunts the Murderers, urging them to show that they are men, not dogs. If they can prove their manhood, he will help them to kill Banquo. The Murderers claim that they are so desperate they'll do anything.*

## 1 Men and dogs (in pairs)

Macbeth taunts the Murderers. Are they just 'men', or do they have particular qualities that mark them out as really worthy? He gives a random list of dogs ('shoughs' and 'water-rugs' are long-haired dogs; 'demi-wolves' are a cross between dogs and wolves). Macbeth then lists some of the dogs' more important qualities ('slow, subtle', and so on).

Try reading lines 91–100 as one long sneer; then explore other ways of speaking them.

## 2 What's made them so bitter? (in groups of three)

Life has embittered the two Murderers (lines 107–13). One doesn't care what he does to spite the world; the other will do anything, even if it results in his death. What has made them like this? Interview the two Murderers (invent their names) for their life stories, to be printed in a popular newspaper.

## 3 Staging the meeting

Work out how to stage the meeting between Macbeth and the Murderers. Is Macbeth seated, or does he walk around the two men? Do the two men stand close together for reassurance, or do they stand apart from each other? Is Macbeth's tone friendly, sinister, threatening, or . . . ?

**so gospelled** such believers in the Christian doctrine of forgiving your enemies
**the catalogue** the list
**clept** called
**valued file** a list arranged by valued qualities
**Particular addition** distinctive qualities
**bill** list, label
**station in the file** place in a list of valued people (or soldiers)

*(Are you going to let this go)*

FIRST MURDERER  You made it known to us.

MACBETH  I did so, and went further, which is now our point of    85   *He Teasing them.*
second meeting. Do you find your patience so predominant in
your nature, that you can let this go? Are you so gospelled, to    *Christian gospelled*
pray for this good man and for his issue, whose heavy hand
*are you going* hath bowed you to the grave and beggared yours forever?

FIRST MURDERER  We are men, my liege.  *loved*    90    *It ('s saying for giving your enemy*

MACBETH  Ay, in the catalogue ye go for men,   *The list*
*For give him* As hounds, and greyhounds, mongrels, spaniels, curs,
Shoughs, water-rugs, and demi-wolves are clept
All by the name of dogs. The valued file
Distinguishes the swift, the slow, the subtle,    95
The housekeeper, the hunter, every one
According to the gift which bounteous nature
Hath in him closed, whereby he does receive
Particular addition from the bill
That writes them all alike. And so of men.    100
Now, if you have a station in the file
Not i'th'worst rank of manhood, say't,
And I will put that business in your bosoms,
Whose execution takes your enemy off,
Grapples you to the heart and love of us    105
Who wear our health but sickly in his life,
Which in his death were perfect.

SECOND MURDERER              I am one, my liege,    *lord*
Whom the vile blows and buffets of the world    *These awful things that happen to these awful things that*
Hath so incensed that I am reckless what I do
To spite the world.

FIRST MURDERER          And I another,
So weary with disasters, tugged with fortune,
That I would set my life on any chance    110    *happen to him*
To mend it or be rid on't.

MACBETH                    Both of you know
Banquo was your enemy.

MURDERERS                  True, my lord.

71

*Macbeth says that Banquo is his enemy, but he cannot kill him openly. He will arrange a time and a place for the Murderers to assassinate Banquo and Fleance so that no suspicion falls upon himself.*

## 1 An invitation to murder (in pairs)

Why doesn't Macbeth simply order the Murderers to do the killing? He is the king and has great power. Instead, he talks with them at some length, and gives some of his reasons. Why?

First, try out several ways of speaking Macbeth's lines opposite (for example, friendly, confidentially, assertively, anxiously). Then write an entry in Macbeth's diary explaining why he didn't merely order the two men to do the murder.

## 2 An interruption

Macbeth cuts off the First Murderer at line 127. How should he speak 'Your spirits shine through you', and what does it suggest about his opinion of the two men?

## 3 Last words?

Compare the final two lines (140–1) with Macbeth's last two lines before he murdered Duncan (Act 2 Scene 1, lines 63–4). Imagine that he intends to kill the two Murderers after they have murdered Banquo. Write two lines in the style of these two couplets which Macbeth could speak to reveal his intention to kill the killers.

## 4 Doing the dirty work (in groups of four or five)

Like all tyrants through the ages, Macbeth hires underlings to do his dirty work for him. Collect examples of such killings today. Talk together about what motivates both the tyrants and the killers.

---

**distance** enmity, quarrel (distance between swordsmen)
**near'st of life** very existence
**bid my will avouch it** justify it by my desires
**the common eye** public view

**perfect spy o'th' time** exact information
**something from** away from
**clearness** freedom from suspicion
**rubs** roughnesses
**botches** bunglings
**material** important

MACBETH  So is he mine, and in such bloody distance                    115
         That every minute of his being thrusts
         Against my near'st of life; and though I could
         With barefaced power sweep him from my sight
         And bid my will avouch it, yet I must not,
         For certain friends that are both his and mine,                120
         Whose loves I may not drop, but wail his fall
         Who I myself struck down. And thence it is
         That I to your assistance do make love,
         Masking the business from the common eye
         For sundry weighty reasons.
SECOND MURDERER                    We shall, my lord,                   125
         Perform what you command us.
FIRST MURDERER                    Though our lives —
MACBETH  Your spirits shine through you. Within this hour at
             most,
         I will advise you where to plant yourselves,
         Acquaint you with the perfect spy o'th'time,
         The moment on't, for't must be done tonight,                   130
         And something from the palace: always thought,
         That I require a clearness. And with him,
         To leave no rubs nor botches in the work,
         Fleance, his son that keeps him company,
         Whose absence is no less material to me                        135
         Than is his father's, must embrace the fate
         Of that dark hour. Resolve yourselves apart,
         I'll come to you anon.
MURDERERS                    We are resolved, my lord.
MACBETH  I'll call upon you straight; abide within.
                                   [Exeunt Murderers]
         It is concluded. Banquo, thy soul's flight,                    140
         If it find heaven, must find it out tonight.             Exit

*Handwritten annotations:* although he can do it / but he's life is on the line. / Hey asking to there help. / The view of the public / we will take your orders / There risking there lives. / where there going / hide. / He the murder to happen to night, / He does not want the murder to be mess up. / get use to it, / They are ready for the killing / want him dead tonight, / Hiding it / many / He needs to be in the palace / murder have.

73

*Lady Macbeth is troubled. She advises Macbeth not to brood on what's done, but he is still racked by fears and insecurity. He even envies the peace of death that Duncan enjoys.*

## 1 Apocalypse now: what dreams? (in pairs)

'Let the frame of things disjoint, both the worlds suffer' says Macbeth, visualising the universe shattering, and heaven and earth in anguish. What are the terrible dreams he has every night? Improvise Macbeth on the psychoanalyst's couch, telling of his dreams.

## 2 'What's done, is done' (in groups of four or five)

Take no notice of things in the past that can't be cured, advises Lady Macbeth. Do you think her advice is sensible and helpful – or even feasible? Talk together about what you would say if that advice were offered to you about something you find worrying. Then discuss whether you think Macbeth can take her advice.

## 3 Uneasy consciences (in pairs)

The rhythms of language can express feelings. Explore lines 4–26 to find as many seesaw rhythms as you can (for example, 'Nought's had, all's spent'). Make a list, then talk together about whether you feel this 'balancing' language (antithesis) catches the uneasiness of conscience that both Macbeths feel. You will find it helpful if you link hands and push and pull as you read to find the movement of the Macbeths' thoughts.

---

**Nought's had, all's spent**
  nothing's gained, everything's lost
**sorriest fancies** miserable
  imaginings
**close, and be herself** join together
  again

**poor malice** weak deeds (to gain
  the crown)
**let the frame of things disjoint**
  let the universe shatter
**Malice domestic** civil war
**foreign levy** foreign armies

# ACT 3   SCENE 2
## A room in Macbeth's palace

*Enter* LADY MACBETH, *and a* SERVANT

LADY MACBETH  Is Banquo gone from court?    *[where they lived is the castle]*
SERVANT  Ay, madam, but returns again tonight.
LADY MACBETH  Say to the king, I would attend his leisure
　　　For a few words.
SERVANT　　　　　　Madam, I will.　　　　　　　　*Exit*
LADY MACBETH　　　　　　　　　　Nought's had, all's spent
　　　Where our desire is got without content.
　　　'Tis safer to be that which we destroy       *[She saying is better to be dead]*   5
　　　Than by destruction dwell in doubtful joy.

*Enter* MACBETH   *[oxymoron]*

　　　How now, my lord, why do you keep alone
　　　Of sorriest fancies your companions making,
　　　Using those thoughts which should indeed have died   *[no point thinking about]*   10
　　　With them they think on? Things without all remedy   *[the dead past]*
　　　Should be without regard; what's done, is done.
MACBETH  We have scorched the snake, not killed it;       *[metaphor what]*
　　　She'll close, and be herself, whilst our poor malice   *[they already]*
　　　Remains in danger of her former tooth.   *[bad intention]*   *[done and]*   15
　　　But let the frame of things disjoint, both the worlds suffer,   *[the danger they]*
　　　Ere we will eat our meal in fear and sleep   *[luck]*
　　　In the affliction of these terrible dreams
　　　That shake us nightly. Better be with the dead   *[He rather be dead.]*
　　　Whom we, to gain our peace, have sent to peace,   20
　　　Than on the torture of the mind to lie
　　　In restless ecstasy. Duncan is in his grave.
　　　After life's fitful fever, he sleeps well;   *[trouble of life]*
　　　Treason has done his worst; nor steel nor poison,
　　　Malice domestic, foreign levy, nothing   *[army]*   25
　　　Can touch him further.

*[Civil war]*

75

*Macbeth tells his wife to pay special regard to Banquo at the banquet. He speaks contemptuously of having to flatter deceitfully. He hints darkly that terrible deeds will be performed that night.*

### 1 Echoes of darkness (in groups of four or five)

Macbeth's lines 40–53 ('ere . . . rouse') have striking similarities to Lady Macbeth's invocation to evil in Act 1 Scene 5, lines 38–52 ('Come . . . hold'). Explore ways of putting together a dramatic presentation of these two appeals to darkness and evil. Which lines 'fit together' most appropriately? Add sound effects.

'O, full of scorpions is my mind, dear wife!' Pick out other lines from this scene that could make a suitable caption for the picture.

---

**Sleek** smooth
**present him eminence** praise and honour him
**unsafe the while** it's still a dangerous time for us
**lave** wash
**vizards** masks

**Nature's copy's not eterne** life doesn't last for ever
**Hecate** goddess of witchcraft
**shard-borne** flying (shard = wing covers)
**seeling** blinding (hawks' eyes were 'seeled' by sewing them up)

LADY MACBETH  Come on. Gentle my lord, *~she~ He wants Macbeth to*
    Sleek o'er your rugged looks, be bright and jovial *be happy,*
    Among your guests tonight.
MACBETH                 So shall I, love,
    And so I pray be you. Let your remembrance       30
    Apply to Banquo, present him eminence *— still dangerous for*
    Both with eye and tongue; unsafe the while, that we *them,*
    Must lave our honours in these flattering streams *~wash~*
    And make our faces vizards to our hearts,
    Disguising what they are. *masks*
LADY MACBETH    *troubled*   You must leave this. *You must stop these*  35
MACBETH  O, full of scorpions is my mind, dear wife!
    Thou know'st that Banquo and his Fleance lives.
LADY MACBETH  But in them Nature's copy's not eterne. *— life doesn't lives forever*
MACBETH  There's comfort yet, they are assailable;
    Then be thou jocund: ere the bat hath flown *Goddess of witches*  40
    His cloistered flight, ere to black Hecate's summons *He a curse on them*
    The shard-borne beetle with his drowsy hums *~The witch~ broken glass*
    Hath rung night's yawning peal, there shall be done
    A deed of dreadful note.
LADY MACBETH           What's to be done?
MACBETH  Be innocent of the knowledge, dearest chuck,     45
    Till thou applaud the deed. Come, seeling night,
    Scarf up the tender eye of pitiful day
    And with thy bloody and invisible hand *blinding night,*
    Cancel and tear to pieces that great bond
    Which keeps me pale. Light thickens, *— image of darkness* 50
    And the crow makes wing to th'rooky wood;
    Good things of day begin to droop and drowse, *go sleep,*
    Whiles night's black agents to their preys do rouse. *bad things happen*
    Thou marvell'st at my words, but hold thee still;
    Things bad begun, make strong themselves by ill. *Rhyming couplet.* 55
    So prithee, go with me.
                       *Exeunt*

*Kill wander about Duncan*

*want you done one bad things you have to continue bad things.*

*worry about me*

*A third Murderer has joined the other two to await their victims. They kill Banquo, but Fleance escapes.*

---

## 1 Act out the scene! (in groups of five)

This very short scene is full of action. It takes place in darkness, but the audience must be able to see exactly what happens. How can you best present it? A hint: slow-motion rehearsals of the attack are helpful, both for working out the movements and for safety.

## 2 Another Murderer? (in small groups)

Why has Macbeth sent along yet another Murderer? Talk together about possible reasons – and about who the Third Murderer might be. Is he one of the other characters in the play? In some productions he is Macbeth himself, in disguise.

## 3 Dying speeches (in groups of three)

In many of his earlier plays, Shakespeare gave long emotional speeches to dying men. But in *Macbeth*, he doesn't do that. Talk together about possible reasons why Shakespeare did not give Duncan and Banquo (and Macbeth himself) dying speeches.

Invent a dying speech for Banquo. Write it in Shakespearian style if you can. Think of all the things Banquo might have said if he'd been given time.

## 4 A poetic murderer?

Some people have found it curious that the First Murderer speaks lines 5–7 ('The west . . . inn'). They feel that such 'poetic' language is inappropriate in the mouth of a common murderer. What do you think?

---

**offices** duties
**To the direction just** precisely
**spurs the lated** gallops the late
**The subject of our watch** the person we are waiting for

**within the note of expectation** on the list of expected guests
**go about** turn back
**best half of our affair** half our reward (or half our task)

# ACT 3   SCENE 3
## A lonely place near Forres

*Enter three* MURDERERS

FIRST MURDERER But who did bid thee join with us?

THIRD MURDERER                                             Macbeth.

SECOND MURDERER He needs not our mistrust, since he delivers
     Our offices and what we have to do
     To the direction just.

FIRST MURDERER [*To Third Murderer*] Then stand with us.
     The west yet glimmers with some streaks of day;       5
     Now spurs the lated traveller apace
     To gain the timely inn and near approaches
     The subject of our watch.

THIRD MURDERER                    Hark, I hear horses.

BANQUO (*within*) Give us a light there, ho!

SECOND MURDERER                          Then 'tis he; the rest
     That are within the note of expectation       10
     Already are i'th'court.

FIRST MURDERER                    His horses go about.

THIRD MURDERER Almost a mile; but he does usually,
     So all men do, from hence to th'palace gate
     Make it their walk.

*Enter* BANQUO *and* FLEANCE, *with a torch*

SECOND MURDERER A light, a light!       15

THIRD MURDERER 'Tis he.

FIRST MURDERER Stand to't.

BANQUO It will be rain tonight.

FIRST MURDERER                    Let it come down.
     [*The Murderers attack. First Murderer strikes out the light*]

BANQUO O, treachery!
     Fly, good Fleance, fly, fly, fly!       20
     Thou mayst revenge – O slave!   [*Dies. Fleance escapes*]

THIRD MURDERER Who did strike out the light?

FIRST MURDERER                          Was't not the way?

THIRD MURDERER There's but one down; the son is fled.

SECOND MURDERER We have lost best half of our affair.

FIRST MURDERER Well, let's away, and say how much is done.    25
                   *Exeunt[, with Banquo's body]*

*Macbeth welcomes his guests to the banquet and mixes with them. The First Murderer reports Banquo's death. The news of Fleance's escape disturbs Macbeth and renews his fears.*

### 1 Changing the scene (in groups of four)

From the darkness of Banquo's murder outside the castle, the scene changes to the bustle of the banqueting hall. How is this scene change managed on stage? Talk together about how to do it effectively and quickly. Remember: you have to get Banquo's body off stage, and you must set up the banquet for the guests.

### 2 The Murderer's report (in pairs)

Work out all the moves for the characters for lines 1–32. Think hard about where and how Macbeth's conversation with the Murderer takes place. What is everyone else on stage doing?

Take parts and experiment with different ways of speaking lines 12–32. Does Macbeth whisper nervously, speak angrily, or does he pretend (to the watching thanes) that it's a normal conversation?

### 3 Free or bound?

The news of Fleance's escape shakes Macbeth to the core. In lines 21–5 he describes a picture of someone free from fear, contrasted with someone tormented by fear. Either draw your own picture, or collect illustrations to show the contrast suggested in Macbeth's words.

### 4 More euphemisms (see page 30)

'Dispatched', 'the like', 'it', 'safe' – once again Macbeth avoids naming the deed murder. Read his lines to the Murderer, substituting – with great emphasis – 'kill' or 'murder' for Macbeth's evasive language.

---

**degrees** status or rank (which determined where they sat at table)
**keeps her state** stays on her throne
**measure** toast
**the nonpareil** without equal

**fit** anxiety
**founded** secure, immovable
**casing** surrounding
**cribbed** shut in a tiny space

# ACT 3 SCENE 4
## The banqueting hall at Forres

Banquet prepared. Two thrones are placed on stage. Enter MACBETH
as King, LADY MACBETH as Queen, ROSS, LENNOX, LORDS, and
attendants. Lady Macbeth sits

MACBETH  You know your own degrees, sit down;
        [*The Lords sit*]
at first and last, the hearty welcome.
LORDS  Thanks to your majesty.
MACBETH  Our self will mingle with society and play the humble       5
host; our hostess keeps her state, but in best time we will
require her welcome.
LADY MACBETH  Pronounce it for me, sir, to all our friends for my
heart speaks, they are welcome.

*Enter* FIRST MURDERER

MACBETH  See, they encounter thee with their hearts' thanks.
    Both sides are even; here I'll sit i'th'midst.       10
    Be large in mirth, anon we'll drink a measure
    The table round. [*To First Murderer*] There's blood upon
    thy face.
FIRST MURDERER  'Tis Banquo's then.
MACBETH  'Tis better thee without, than he within.
    Is he dispatched?       15
FIRST MURDERER  My lord, his throat is cut; that I did for him.
MACBETH  Thou art the best o'th'cut-throats,
    Yet he's good that did the like for Fleance;
    If thou didst it, thou art the nonpareil.
FIRST MURDERER  Most royal sir, Fleance is scaped.       20
MACBETH  Then comes my fit again: I had else been perfect;
    Whole as the marble, founded as the rock,
    As broad and general as the casing air:
    But now I am cabined, cribbed, confined, bound in
    To saucy doubts and fears. But Banquo's safe?       25
FIRST MURDERER  Ay, my good lord: safe in a ditch he bides,
    With twenty trenchèd gashes on his head,
    The least a death to nature.

81

*Macbeth consoles himself that Fleance is too young to do harm yet. Lady Macbeth bids him welcome his guests. The sight of Banquo's Ghost unnerves Macbeth. Lady Macbeth attempts to calm the Lords.*

## 1 The Ghost of Banquo: seen or unseen? (in pairs)

Every time the play is produced, the director must decide whether or not to bring on a Ghost that the audience can see. Of all the characters on stage, only Macbeth sees the Ghost. In Shakespeare's time, and in the eighteenth and nineteenth centuries, the audience was shown the Ghost, but in the second half of the twentieth century, some productions have left it to the audience's imagination.

Talk together about the advantages and disadvantages of an invisible Ghost. If you argue for having an actor play the Ghost, what does he look like, what does he wear, how does he move? One Ghost in a production in the 1980s was so drenched in blood that the audience simply found him funny.

## 2 Ceremony (in small groups)

Lady Macbeth's lines 32–7 are formal and ceremonious. She reminds Macbeth to welcome his guests ('give the cheer'), because without such welcoming toasts, it would merely be a paid-for meal ('sold'). Eating in company away from home should be enriched by such ceremony. Talk together about 'the sauce to meat is ceremony'. Find modern examples that illustrate the phrase.

## 3 'Our country's honour roofed' (in groups of six to ten)

If only Banquo were here, says Macbeth, all the nobility of Scotland would be under our roof. Who would be included? Invent your own list of thanes and their wives and other guests. Draw up a stage plan showing the seating arrangements. Make sure the audience can see everyone.

---

**grown serpent** that is, Banquo
**worm** that is, Fleance
**give the cheer** welcome your guests
**is sold ... without it** unless there are many ceremonious welcomes, it's like a take-away meal

**Who may ... mischance** I hope he's absent because of unkindness rather than an accident
**gory locks** blood-covered hair
**much you note him** you watch him closely

MACBETH                    Thanks for that.
There the grown serpent lies; the worm that's fled
Hath nature that in time will venom breed,—            30
No teeth for th'present. Get thee gone; tomorrow
We'll hear ourselves again,        *Exit [First] Murderer*
LADY MACBETH              My royal lord,
You do not give the cheer; the feast is sold
That is not often vouched while 'tis a-making
'Tis given with welcome. To feed were best at home:   35
From thence, the sauce to meat is ceremony,
Meeting were bare without it.

*Enter the* GHOST OF BANQUO *and sits in Macbeth's place*

MACBETH                         Sweet remembrancer!
Now good digestion wait on appetite,
And health on both.
LENNOX                    May't please your highness, sit.
MACBETH  Here had we now our country's honour roofed,   40
Were the graced person of our Banquo present,
Who may I rather challenge for unkindness
Than pity for mischance.
ROSS                         His absence, sir,
Lays blame upon his promise. Please't your highness
To grace us with your royal company?                    45
MACBETH  The table's full.
LENNOX                    Here is a place reserved, sir.
MACBETH  Where?
LENNOX  Here, my good lord. What is't that moves your highness?
MACBETH  Which of you have done this?
LORDS                         What, my good lord?
MACBETH  Thou canst not say I did it; never shake        50
Thy gory locks at me!
ROSS  Gentlemen, rise, his highness is not well.
              [*Lady Macbeth joins the Lords*]
LADY MACBETH  Sit, worthy friends. My lord is often thus,
And hath been from his youth. Pray you, keep seat.
The fit is momentary; upon a thought                     55
He will again be well. If much you note him
You shall offend him and extend his passion.
Feed, and regard him not. [*To Macbeth*] Are you a man?

83

*Lady Macbeth rebukes Macbeth for his display of fear. The Ghost leaves. Macbeth broods on how the dead return. He recovers his composure, reassures the thanes and proposes a toast. The Ghost re-enters.*

### 1 Whispering (in pairs)

Much of lines 58–83 ('Are you . . . murder is') is an intensely private conversation (even though the startled thanes must be eager to listen to what is being said). No one must hear the incriminating words about the dagger, or Duncan, or murders. Sit close together and whisper the lines to each other. Change characters and repeat. Work out how the audience would hear the conversation, but the banquet guests would not.

'Prithee, see there! Behold, look, lo!' Macbeth challenges the Ghost to speak, believing he has returned from a charnel house (storehouse for the bones of the dead). But Lady Macbeth and the guests can see only an empty chair. Write down several reasons why only Macbeth can see the Ghost. Compare your reasons with those of other students.

---

**O proper stuff!** rubbish!
**flaws and starts** sudden tantrums
**Impostors to** false in comparison with
**grandam** grandmother
**monuments** graves

**maws of kites** stomachs of birds of prey
**Ere humane statute purged** before law banished evil from
**weal** commonwealth
**muse** wonder

MACBETH  Ay, and a bold one, that dare look on that
Which might appal the devil.
LADY MACBETH                    O proper stuff!                    60
This is the very painting of your fear;
This is the air-drawn dagger which you said
Led you to Duncan. O, these flaws and starts,
Impostors to true fear, would well become
A woman's story at a winter's fire                                65
Authorised by her grandam. Shame itself!
Why do you make such faces? When all's done
You look but on a stool.
MACBETH  Prithee, see there! Behold, look, lo! How say you?
[To Ghost] Why, what care I? If thou canst nod, speak too.   70
If charnel houses and our graves must send
Those that we bury back, our monuments
Shall be the maws of kites.
                              [Exit Ghost of Banquo]
LADY MACBETH            What, quite unmanned in folly?
MACBETH  If I stand here, I saw him.
LADY MACBETH                    Fie, for shame.
MACBETH  Blood hath been shed ere now, i'th'olden time,    75
Ere humane statute purged the gentle weal;
Ay, and since too, murders have been performed
Too terrible for the ear. The time has been
That when the brains were out, the man would die,
And there an end. But now they rise again                      80
With twenty mortal murders on their crowns
And push us from our stools. This is more strange
Than such a murder is.
LADY MACBETH            My worthy lord,
Your noble friends do lack you.
MACBETH                    I do forget –
Do not muse at me, my most worthy friends.                    85
I have a strange infirmity which is nothing
To those that know me. Come, love and health to all,
Then I'll sit down. Give me some wine; fill full!

                Enter GHOST [OF BANQUO]

I drink to th'general joy o'th'whole table,

*Macbeth, his composure recovered, proposes a toast to Banquo and the guests. On seeing the Ghost again he bursts into violent language, commanding him away. Lady Macbeth orders the Lords to leave.*

## 1 Second appearance! (in small groups)

Work out how the Ghost enters and how he behaves during Macbeth's violent outbursts (lines 89–107).

## 2 Banishing a ghost (whole class – a noisy activity!)

To experience the power of Macbeth's language, divide the class in two. The two groups face each other across the room. Take lines 93–107 and, in turn, hurl a short section at each other:

Group 1: Avaunt and quit my sight!
Group 2: Let the earth hide thee!
Group 1: Thy bones are marrowless, thy blood is cold.

Accompany your sentences with appropriate gestures.

## 3 'What sights, my lord?'

The guests at the banquet are amazed at Macbeth's strange behaviour. Ross asks a question: 'What sights, my lord?' (line 116) that expresses their suspicions – what is it that Macbeth is seeing? As director of the play, advise everyone present on stage at this moment just how (and why) they should behave as they hear Ross's question.

## 4 'Stand not upon the order of your going'
(in groups of six to eight)

Lady Macbeth orders the guests to leave immediately without any thought of precedence or rank (usually the most senior would leave first). Make up a mime based on lines 1 and 119.

---

**Our ... pledge** here's to our homage and the toast
**speculation** sight
**peers** lords, thanes
**Hyrcan tiger** savage tiger (supposed to live in Hyrcania, near the Caspian Sea)

**If trembling ... girl** if I tremble, call me a girl
**admired** wondered at
**strange ... owe** wonder if I really am courageous
**blanched** white

And to our dear friend Banquo, whom we miss. *— offering a* 90
Would he were here! To all, and him we thirst, *— toast about banquo*
And all to all.

LORDS                              Our duties and the pledge. *— cheers!*

MACBETH  Avaunt and quit my sight! Let the earth hide thee!
*talking to banquo* Thy bones are marrowless, thy blood is cold;
*nervous mirror?* Thou hast no speculation in those eyes— *there no eyes you* 95
Which thou dost glare with. *stare at me*

LADY MACBETH                    Think of this, good peers,
But as a thing of custom. 'Tis no other, *— not serious but spoils the*
Only it spoils the pleasure of the time. *— time (the party)*

MACBETH  What man dare, I dare; *I am as brave as any man*
Approach thou like the rugged Russian bear,              100
The armed rhinoceros, or th'Hyrcan tiger,
Take any shape but that, and my firm nerves
Shall never tremble. Or be alive again,
And dare me to the desert with thy sword;
If trembling I inhabit then, protest me                    105
*you could call me a girl* The baby of a girl. Hence horrible shadow, *macbeth's imagination*
Unreal mock'ry hence.

                        [*Exit Ghost of Banquo*]
                    Why so, being gone,
I am a man again. – Pray you, sit still.

LADY MACBETH  You have displaced the mirth, broke the good
        meeting        *— you ruined the party*
With most admired disorder.

MACBETH                          Can such things be,                110
And overcome us like a summer's cloud, *— you without strange wonder*
Without our special wonder? You make me strange *wonder if he's brave*
Even to the disposition that I owe,
When now I think you can behold such sights
And keep the natural ruby of your cheeks,                  115
When mine is blanched with fear. *— goes pale in fear*

ROSS                              What sights, my lord? *— what are you talking about*

LADY MACBETH  I pray you speak not; he grows worse and worse.
Question enrages him. At once, good night.
Stand not upon the order of your going,
But go at once.

*The Lords leave. Macbeth broods on murder and unnaturalness. He vows to visit the Witches to know his future, swearing that from now on there is no turning back. He will kill anyone standing in his way.*

## 1 'Blood will have blood'

*Either*: make up a poem of four or five verses in which each verse ends 'blood will have blood'.

*Or*: illustrate the image of Macbeth wading half-way across a river of blood.

## 2 'It will have blood . . .' (in groups of three or four)

Explore ways of turning lines 122–6 into an incantation by the three weird sisters. Use repetition and choral speaking. Inter-cut them with some of the Witches' lines. Chant your final version as an echo for Macbeth as he speaks the rest of his lines.

## 3 'For mine own good . . .' (in large groups)

Guilt gives way to determination to act. Macbeth will now do any act, however evil, that furthers his own interest. He leaves, saying that his illusion of seeing Banquo's Ghost is only the fear of a beginner who needs experience. Talk together about whether there is any redeeming feature of anyone who can say 'For mine own good, /All causes shall give way'. Isn't that the attitude of every tyrant in every age?

## 4 A thirty-second banquet (in groups of six to eight)

Speeded-up versions can help you to identify the major points of action in a scene. Work out a thirty-second presentation of the whole scene. Which group can show the fullest version in thirty seconds?

---

**Augures, and understood relations** prophecies, and meaningful patterns
**maggot-pies, and choughs** magpies and birds like crows
**denies his person /At** absents himself from

**a servant feed** a paid spy
**worst means** most evil methods
**acted . . . scanned** done at once without thought
**initiate** inexperienced, first

LENNOX          Good night, and better health          120
          Attend his majesty.
LADY MACBETH          A kind good night to all.
          *Exeunt Lords and Attendants*
MACBETH  It will have blood they say: blood will have blood. —*If you kill someone*
          Stones have been known to move and trees to speak. *there will kill you*
          Augures, and understood relations, have
          By maggot-pies, and choughs, and rooks brought forth          125
          The secret'st man of blood. What is the night? — *what time is it,*
LADY MACBETH  Almost at odds with morning, which is which.
MACBETH  How sayst thou that Macduff denies his person
          At our great bidding?
LADY MACBETH          Did you send to him, sir?
MACBETH  I hear it by the way, but I will send. *Servant in every house and he sent*          130
          There's not a one of them but in his house          *letter.*
          I keep a servant feed. I will tomorrow –
          And betimes I will – to the weïrd sisters. *witches*
          More shall they speak. For now I am bent to know          *I want to know what*
          By the worst means, the worst; for mine own good,          *the worst thing*          135
          All causes shall give way. I am in blood          *that can happen,*
          Stepped in so far that should I wade no more, *I have done so many*
          Returning were as tedious as go o'er.          *bad things I am so carried*
          Strange things I have in head that will to hand,          *in blood that it is*
          Which must be acted ere they may be scanned.          *as easy to carry on*          140
LADY MACBETH  You lack the season of all natures, sleep.
MACBETH  Come, we'll to sleep. My strange and self-abuse          *you need to*
          Is the initiate fear that wants hard use;          *sleep*
          We are yet but young in deed.
          *we only started          Exeunt*
          *the killing* 
          *people death*
          *sleep is*
          *Inexperienced, first,*

89

*Hecate rebukes the Witches for speaking to Macbeth without involving her. She bids them meet her at the pit of Acheron to tell Macbeth his destiny. She promises to use magic to ruin the over-confident Macbeth.*

## 1 Is it by Shakespeare? (in pairs or groups of three)

There have been many arguments about whether Shakespeare himself wrote this scene. Take turns to read it aloud to each other sharing the language as follows:

First reading: a line at a time
Second reading: up to a punctuation mark
Third reading: in sections that make sense to you.

Then talk together about whether you think it is by Shakespeare. Compare your answer and reasons with other groups.

## 2 How to perform it? (in groups of four)

This scene is often cut in stage performances. Imagine that you have decided to include it. How will you stage it, and what will your Hecate look like?

## 3 Find the lines

Identify the sections in lines 2–35 that match the following parts of Hecate's meaning: (i) reasons for anger; (ii) self-centred Macbeth; (iii) meet tomorrow with spells; (iv) I'm off to collect moon-vapour for magic to ruin Macbeth; (v) Macbeth's future; (vi) My spirit calls.

## 4 'Security': a change of meaning

The meaning of 'security' (line 32) has changed. In Shakespeare's time it meant 'being over-confident' or 'lacking anxiety'. That seems to describe the Macbeth at the end of Act 3 Scene 4. He no longer worries that the evil deeds he intends will result in the damnation of his soul.

---

**Hecate** goddess of witchcraft
**beldams** hags
**close contriver** secret maker
**Acheron** a river in Hell
**vap'rous drop profound** magical
  potion

**sleights** tricks
**artificial sprites** apparitions, false
  spirits
**security** over-confidence

# ACT 3   SCENE 5
## A desolate place

Thunder. Enter the three WITCHES, meeting HECATE

FIRST WITCH  Why how now, Hecate, you look angerly?
HECATE  Have I not reason, beldams, as you are,
       Saucy and over-bold? How did you dare
       To trade and traffic with Macbeth
       In riddles and affairs of death?                          5
       And I the mistress of your charms,
       The close contriver of all harms,
       Was never called to bear my part
       Or show the glory of our art?
       And which is worse, all you have done                     10
       Hath been but for a wayward son,
       Spiteful and wrathful, who, as others do,
       Loves for his own ends, not for you.
       But make amends now. Get you gone,
       And at the pit of Acheron                                 15
       Meet me i'th'morning. Thither he
       Will come to know his destiny.
       Your vessels and your spells provide,
       Your charms and every thing beside.
       I am for th'air. This night I'll spend                    20
       Unto a dismal and a fatal end.
       Great business must be wrought ere noon.
       Upon the corner of the moon
       There hangs a vap'rous drop profound;
       I'll catch it ere it come to ground;                      25
       And that distilled by magic sleights,
       Shall raise such artificial sprites
       As by the strength of their illusion
       Shall draw him on to his confusion.
       He shall spurn fate, scorn death, and bear               30
       His hopes 'bove wisdom, grace, and fear.
       And you all know, security
       Is mortals' chiefest enemy.

*Lennox comments guardedly and ironically on Macbeth's guilt as he recounts the killing of Duncan, Banquo and the grooms. He hints at Macbeth's murderous intentions towards Malcolm, Donaldbain and Fleance.*

## 1 Language and tyranny (in pairs)

Under a dictatorship, everyone must watch their language. It's dangerous to voice your thoughts openly. Turn Lennox's lines 1–24 into a conversation. You'll find that it works well as a carefully guarded conversation where both speakers are afraid to speak the truth plainly. Practise different ways of sharing the lines.

Afterwards, improvise a conversation between two citizens in a totalitarian state, testing each other to find if they are allies in the cause of freedom.

Hitler and Stalin were tyrants who, like Macbeth, ruled by fear, suppressing free speech and opposition. In Nazi Germany and the Communist Soviet Union, men and women had to be as guarded in their speech as Lennox. Spies and informers were always around to betray those who spoke openly.

---

**but hit your thoughts** echoed your own beliefs
**strangely borne** oddly carried out
**marry** indeed (by St Mary)
**too late** at night

**want the thought** fail to think
**thralls** prisoners
**under his key** within his power
**broad words** frank talk
**bestows himself** lives now

*Music, and a song* ['*Come away, come away*', *within*]
>Hark, I am called: my little spirit, see,
>Sits in a foggy cloud, and stays for me.                    [*Exit*]    35
FIRST WITCH  Come, let's make haste; she'll soon be back again.

*Exeunt*

# ACT 3    SCENE 6
## The castle of Lennox

*Enter* LENNOX *and another* LORD

LENNOX  My former speeches have but hit your thoughts
>Which can interpret further; only I say
>Things have been strangely borne. The gracious Duncan
>Was pitied of Macbeth; marry, he was dead.
>And the right-valiant Banquo walked too late,                5
>Whom you may say, if't please you, Fleance killed,
>For Fleance fled. Men must not walk too late.
>Who cannot want the thought how monstrous
>It was for Malcolm and for Donaldbain
>To kill their gracious father? Damnèd fact,                 10
>How it did grieve Macbeth! Did he not straight
>In pious rage the two delinquents tear,
>That were the slaves of drink and thralls of sleep?
>Was not that nobly done? Ay, and wisely too,
>For 'twould have angered any heart alive                    15
>To hear the men deny't. So that I say,
>He has borne all things well, and I do think
>That had he Duncan's sons under his key –
>As, an't please heaven, he shall not – they should find
>What 'twere to kill a father. So should Fleance.            20
>But peace, for from broad words and 'cause he failed
>His presence at the tyrant's feast, I hear
>Macduff lives in disgrace. Sir, can you tell
>Where he bestows himself?

*The unnamed Lord tells of Malcolm's warm welcome in England, and of
Macduff's plea to King Edward for an army to overthrow Macbeth's
tyranny. He reports Macduff's refusal to visit Macbeth.*

## 1 Who is the unnamed Lord?

The unnamed Lord has a similar dramatic function to the Old Man
of Act 2 Scene 4, who represented the ordinary people of Scotland.
His words are of hope and eventual peace. Do you think he should
have a name, or remain as a representative voice, like a chorus?

## 2 'Our suffering country' (in groups of six)

Lines 34–6 describe all that is absent in Scotland under Macbeth's
tyrannical rule. Identify the five elements in the lines and make five
tableaux, each of which shows 'present Scotland' and 'future
Scotland'.

## 3 'The cloudy messenger' (in pairs)

In several Shakespeare plays, the messenger who brings bad news
gets into trouble merely for reporting it. Macbeth's 'cloudy messenger' of lines 41–4 is obviously resentful of Macduff's refusal to return
to Scotland. It will hinder ('clog') the messenger's career prospects.

Imagine that you are the messenger. You are travelling back to
Macbeth's castle with the bad news of Macduff's answer. Work out a
story that tells the truth but that you hope will avoid your being
punished by Macbeth.

## 4 Good and evil (in groups of three)

One person quietly reads aloud the whole scene. Another echoes
every word to do with evil or wrongdoing (for example, 'strangely',
'deed'). The third person echoes every word to do with goodness,
hope or Heaven (for example, 'gracious', 'right-valiant').

---

**holds the due of birth** steals his
  birthright, the crown
**the most pious Edward** King
  Edward the Confessor (reigned
  1042–66)
**with such grace . . . respect** with full
  dignity, despite the loss of his throne

**pray** request
**him above** God
**ratify** justify
**cloudy** sullen
**hums** mutters
**to a caution** to be careful

LORD                              The son of Duncan,
       From whom this tyrant holds the due of birth,                      25
       Lives in the English court and is received
       Of the most pious Edward with such grace,
       That the malevolence of fortune nothing
       Takes from his high respect. Thither Macduff
       Is gone to pray the holy king upon his aid                         30
       To wake Northumberland and warlike Siward
       That by the help of these, with him above
       To ratify the work, we may again
       Give to our tables meat, sleep to our nights,
       Free from our feasts and banquets bloody knives,                   35
       Do faithful homage and receive free honours,
       All which we pine for now. And this report
       Hath so exasperate their king that he
       Prepares for some attempt of war.
LENNOX  Sent he to Macduff?                                               40
LORD  He did. And with an absolute, 'Sir, not I',
       The cloudy messenger turns me his back
       And hums, as who should say, 'You'll rue the time
       That clogs me with this answer.'
LENNOX                               And that well might
       Advise him to a caution t'hold what distance                       45
       His wisdom can provide. Some holy angel
       Fly to the court of England and unfold
       His message ere he come, that a swift blessing
       May soon return to this our suffering country
       Under a hand accursed.
LORD                        I'll send my prayers with him.                50
                                                     *Exeunt*

# Looking back at Act 3
*Activities for groups or individuals*

## 1 The coronation of Macbeth

Act 3 opens shortly after Macbeth has been crowned at Scone as High King of Scotland. The scene is not shown in the play.

*Either*: invent a suitable coronation ceremony for the new king and queen. You will need words and actions of great ritual and formality to match the importance of the event.

*Or*: write an account of the coronation as seen by a participant.

Begin your story by stating which character you are (you can be an actual character in the play or an invented one).

## 2 Act summary

Write six sentences, one for each scene, summarising the action.

## 3 The voice of conscience

Macbeth and Lady Macbeth have got what they wanted, but it has not brought happiness. Macbeth is tortured by his conscience, and although Lady Macbeth tries to comfort him, she too is racked with anxiety ('Nought's had, all's spent'). They have achieved their ambition at great cost. Improvise a modern parallel where a husband and wife achieve great power and status by evil means and suffer the psychological consequences.

## 4 Memorable lines

Pick out one line from each scene that makes a strong impression on you. Write them down, then compare your chosen lines with those of other students. Discuss the reasons for your choices.

## 5 A changing relationship

Act 3 is the last time the Macbeths are seen together. It also marks the point where their relationship changes. Previously, Lady Macbeth has been the leader, prompting Macbeth to the murder of Duncan. Identify each time she appears in this act, and write several sentences describing how her relationship with her husband changes.

## 6  A speaking Ghost?

Banquo's Ghost does not speak. Prepare two short speeches, in Shakespearian style, for the Ghost. Identify appropriate places in the script to insert them.

## 7  Is war justified?

The act ends with Lennox invoking the help of Heaven. His words imply that England should come to Scotland's aid and overthrow Macbeth by violence. Do you think that such armed struggle is justified or whether there is such a thing as 'a just war'?

## 8  'Good things of day begin to droop and drowse'

One critic thought that this line was 'the motto of the entire tragedy'. Use the line as inspiration to design a poster advertising a production.

## 9  Spies

Macbeth has set up a network of paid spies ('a servant fee'd') in the households of all his thanes. Write a report by one of the spies (who thinks that the more sensational the report, the greater the fee).

## 10  A disastrous evening (in groups of six or seven)

Use the banquet scene as a source of ideas to improvise a party that goes disastrously wrong. The host behaves strangely. His wife tries to keep the party going normally.

## 11  What happened?

The thanes are abruptly dismissed from the banquet in Scene 4. Take parts as some of the guests and develop a conversation about what you think happened at the banquet, and what you think about it.

## 12  Macbeth's coat of arms

Monarchs have a heraldic device: a picture (or coat of arms). It symbolises their power and depicts in some way their perception of themselves and their nations. Design Macbeth's coat of arms.

## 13  'Gentle my lord', 'dearest chuck'

Make a collection of all the different ways the Macbeths have addressed each other so far. Do you think they truly love each other?

*The Witches prepare to meet Macbeth. They chant as they circle the cauldron, throwing in horrible ingredients to make a sickening brew.*

---

### 1 Act it out! (in groups of three or more)

Work out the most effective way to stage lines 1–38. You'll find that you can quickly learn the lines. If you work in a group larger than three, share the lines out so that everyone speaks four or five times. You'll find that several people speaking together can add to the dramatic effect.

### 2 An ecological view (in pairs)

Shakespeare's Witches regarded certain animals and reptiles as evil. Today, many people regard them quite differently – not as evil, but as our fellow creatures on earth. One person reads lines 1–38. The other, as an ecologist, interrupts after each animal or reptile is mentioned, to explain their 'good' aspects. Here are some explanations to help you (others are given at the foot of the page):

*hedge-pig*   hedgehog
*blind-worm*   slow-worm
*howlet*   young owl
*mummy*   mummified corpse
*hemlock*   poisonous plant
*yew*   poisonous tree

### 3 Invent your own recipe: hellish or divine

Make a hell-broth of your own by thinking up your own ingredients. Use the same rhythms as the Witches. What difference does it make if you invent a 'divine-stew' made with pleasant ingredients?

---

**brindled** streaked with colour
**Harpier** name of a familiar (a harpy had a woman's face and a bird's body); (see page 2)
**Sweltered venom** poisonous sweat
**fenny** slimy
**maw and gulf** stomach and throat

**ravined** full of devoured prey
**Jew ... Turk ... Tartar** all non-Christians
**drab** prostitute
**slab** sticky
**chawdron** entrails, stomach

# ACT 4  SCENE I
## A desolate place near Forres

*Thunder. Enter the three WITCHES*

FIRST WITCH  Thrice the brindled cat hath mewed.
SECOND WITCH  Thrice and once the hedge-pig whined.
THIRD WITCH  Harpier cries, ''Tis time, 'tis time.'
FIRST WITCH  Round about the cauldron go;
    In the poisoned entrails throw.                     5
    Toad, that under cold stone
    Days and nights has thirty-one
    Sweltered venom sleeping got,
    Boil thou first i'th'charmèd pot.
ALL  Double, double toil and trouble;            10
    Fire burn, and cauldron bubble.
SECOND WITCH  Fillet of a fenny snake,
    In the cauldron boil and bake:
    Eye of newt, and toe of frog,
    Wool of bat, and tongue of dog,              15
    Adder's fork, and blind-worm's sting,
    Lizard's leg, and howlet's wing,
    For a charm of powerful trouble,
    Like a hell-broth, boil and bubble.
ALL  Double, double toil and trouble,            20
    Fire burn, and cauldron bubble.
THIRD WITCH  Scale of dragon, tooth of wolf,
    Witches' mummy, maw and gulf
    Of the ravined salt-sea shark,
    Root of hemlock, digged i'th'dark;         25
    Liver of blaspheming Jew,
    Gall of goat, and slips of yew,
    Slivered in the moon's eclipse;
    Nose of Turk, and Tartar's lips,
    Finger of birth-strangled babe,           30
    Ditch-delivered by a drab,
    Make the gruel thick and slab.
    Add thereto a tiger's chawdron
    For th'ingredience of our cauldron.

*The Witches complete the preparation of their hellish brew and are congratulated by Hecate. Macbeth enters and challenges them to answer what he asks, irrespective of the most appalling consequences.*

### 1 'Black spirits'

The words of the song appear in *The Witches*, a play by Thomas Middleton (a contemporary of Shakespeare). Invent your own words to fit the title 'Black spirits'. Catch the atmosphere of the cauldron scene!

### 2 Tell me – though destruction follows! (in groups of six)

Macbeth is obsessed with one thought: the desire to know the future. He appeals to the Witches to answer him even if the result is the destruction of the world. His language is like that of the Witches: 'I conjure you' is the beginning of a spell or incantation. Try one or more of these activities on lines 49–60:

a one person whispers them; everyone else echoes every 'though'
b speak them round the group as a witch-like spell
c share them out; create appropriate sound effects for each section
d make six 'pictures' (for example, drawings, paintings, tableaux) to show each element of Macbeth's imaginings of the destruction that follows each 'though'
e inter-cut lines 51–9 with *King Lear* Act 3 Scene 2, lines 1–9.

### 3 'Though bladed corn be lodged' (line 54)

Witches were believed to have the power to move corn from place to place, or to flatten it. That superstition still lingers. All over southern England in the summer of 1990 'corn circles' appeared, that is, corn, flattened into elaborate shapes. Though many people believe that corn circles are an elaborate hoax, many others believe that they are the work of extra-terrestrial beings.

---

**yeasty** frothy
**navigation** shipping
**bladed . . . lodged** growing corn is flattened

**warders** owners, keepers
**slope** bend
**nature's germen** the seeds of all life

ALL Double, double toil and trouble,                          35
     Fire burn, and cauldron bubble.
SECOND WITCH Cool it with a baboon's blood,
     Then the charm is firm and good.

*Enter* HECATE, *and the other three Witches*

HECATE O well done! I commend your pains,
     And every one shall share i'th'gains;                  40
     And now about the cauldron sing
     Like elves and fairies in a ring,
     Enchanting all that you put in.
        *Music, and a song, 'Black spirits, etc.'*
        *[Exeunt Hecate and the other three Witches]*
SECOND WITCH By the pricking of my thumbs,
     Something wicked this way comes;                        45
     Open locks, whoever knocks.

*Enter* MACBETH

MACBETH How now, you secret, black, and midnight hags!
     What is't you do?
ALL THE WITCHES      A deed without a name.
MACBETH I conjure you by that which you profess,
     Howe'er you come to know it, answer me.                 50
     Though you untie the winds and let them fight
     Against the churches, though the yeasty waves
     Confound and swallow navigation up,
     Though bladed corn be lodged and trees blown down,
     Though castles topple on their warders' heads,          55
     Though palaces and pyramids do slope
     Their heads to their foundations, though the treasure
     Of nature's germen tumble altogether
     Even till destruction sicken: answer me
     To what I ask you.
FIRST WITCH      Speak.
SECOND WITCH      Demand.
THIRD WITCH      We'll answer.                              60
FIRST WITCH Say, if thou'dst rather hear it from our mouths,
     Or from our masters'?
MACBETH      Call 'em, let me see 'em.

*The Witches show their Apparitions. An armed Head warns Macbeth: 'beware Macduff'. A bloody Child tells him that no naturally born man can harm him. Macbeth, though reassured, swears to kill Macduff.*

The Witches show one of the Apparitions.

Rehearse a presentation of lines 60–93. The three Apparitions are invitations to exercise your imagination. No one knows for sure quite what they look like: 'an armed Head', 'a bloody Child', 'a Child crowned, with a tree in his hand'. In Shakespeare's theatre they probably appeared through a trapdoor. Stage your own entries however you think fit.

**farrow** litter of piglets
**the murderer's gibbet** where a murderer was hanged
**office** function, purpose
**deftly** skilfully
**harped** echoed
**potent** powerful

**assurance double sure** my security even more sure
**take a bond of fate** swear a binding oath
**issue** descendant, child
**the round /And top of sovereignty** the crown

FIRST WITCH Pour in sow's blood, that hath eaten
    Her nine farrow; grease that's sweaten
    From the murderer's gibbet throw     65
    Into the flame.
ALL THE WITCHES Come high or low:
    Thyself and office deftly show.

  *Thunder. [Enter]* FIRST APPARITION, *an armed Head*

MACBETH Tell me, thou unknown power –
FIRST WITCH        He knows thy thought;
    Hear his speech, but say thou nought.
FIRST APPARITION Macbeth, Macbeth, Macbeth: beware
    Macduff,             70
    Beware the Thane of Fife. Dismiss me. Enough. *Descends*
MACBETH Whate'er thou art, for thy good caution, thanks;
    Thou hast harped my fear aright. But one word more –
FIRST WITCH He will not be commanded. Here's another,
    More potent than the first.       75

  *Thunder. [Enter]* SECOND APPARITION, *a bloody Child*

SECOND APPARITION Macbeth, Macbeth, Macbeth.
MACBETH Had I three ears, I'd hear thee.
SECOND APPARITION Be bloody, bold, and resolute; laugh to
    scorn
    The power of man, for none of woman born
    Shall harm Macbeth.     *Descends* 80
MACBETH Then live, Macduff, what need I fear of thee?
    But yet I'll make assurance double sure
    And take a bond of fate: thou shalt not live,
    That I may tell pale-hearted fear it lies,
    And sleep in spite of thunder.

  *Thunder. [Enter]* THIRD APPARITION, *a Child crowned, with a tree*
      *in his hand*

          What is this,   85
    That rises like the issue of a king
    And wears upon his baby-brow the round
    And top of sovereignty?
ALL THE WITCHES    Listen, but speak not to't.

*The Third Apparition promises that Macbeth will not be defeated until Birnam Wood comes to Dunsinane. Macbeth demands to know more about the future. The Witches present a procession of eight kings and Banquo.*

## 1 A show of eight kings

Many believe that Shakespeare had James I and the Stuarts very much in mind as he wrote the play (see page 165). The eight kings are the ancestors of King James I of England. He saw *Macbeth* shortly after it was written. One story is that the eighth king carried a mirror ('glass') and, at line 118, focused it on the watching King James. All England's present royalty descends from James, so Macbeth really would see 'many more' in the mirror.

The 'two-fold balls and treble sceptres' could also be a flattering reference to King James. They represent the two orbs he carried at his two coronations in Scotland and England, and the three kingdoms he now ruled: Scotland, England and Ireland.

Work in groups of nine to ten. As one person speaks lines 111–23, your audience should see appropriate images of the kings and Banquo.

An eighteenth-century version of a show of eight kings.

**lion-mettled** courageous
**Who chafes ... frets ...**
  **conspirers** rebels, dissidents
**impress** conscript
**bodements** prophecies
**the lease of nature** the length of natural life

**mortal custom** usual life-span
**sear** burn
**th'crack of doom** doomsday, the thunder of the Day of Judgement
**blood-boltered** spattered in blood

THIRD APPARITION  Be lion-mettled, proud, and take no care
          Who chafes, who frets, or where conspirers are.                    90
          Macbeth shall never vanquished be until
          Great Birnam Wood to high Dunsinane hill
          Shall come against him.                        *Descends*
MACBETH                        That will never be:
          Who can impress the forest, bid the tree
          Unfix his earthbound root? Sweet bodements, good.              95
          Rebellious dead, rise never till the wood
          Of Birnam rise, and our high-placed Macbeth
          Shall live the lease of nature, pay his breath
          To time and mortal custom. Yet my heart
          Throbs to know one thing. Tell me, if your art               100
          Can tell so much, shall Banquo's issue ever
          Reign in this kingdom?
ALL THE WITCHES              Seek to know no more.
MACBETH  I will be satisfied. Deny me this,
          And an eternal curse fall on you. Let me know.
                  [*Cauldron descends.*] *Hautboys*
          Why sinks that cauldron? And what noise is this?              105
FIRST WITCH  Show!
SECOND WITCH  Show!
THIRD WITCH  Show!
ALL THE WITCHES  Show his eyes and grieve his heart,
          Come like shadows, so depart.                                 110
    [*Enter*] *a show of eight kings, and* [*the*] *last with a glass in his hand*[;
              *Banquo's Ghost following*]
MACBETH  Thou art too like the spirit of Banquo. Down!
          Thy crown does sear mine eyeballs. And thy hair,
          Thou other gold-bound brow, is like the first;
          A third, is like the former. – Filthy hags,
          Why do you show me this? – A fourth? Start, eyes!             115
          What, will the line stretch out to th'crack of doom?
          Another yet? A seventh? I'll see no more.
          And yet the eighth appears, who bears a glass
          Which shows me many more. And some I see,
          That two-fold balls and treble sceptres carry.                120
          Horrible sight! Now I see 'tis true,
          For the blood-boltered Banquo smiles upon me,
          And points at them for his.
              [*Exeunt show of kings and Banquo's Ghost*]
                  What, is this so?

*Having presented Banquo's descendants as kings, the Witches dance, then vanish, to Macbeth's anger. Hearing of Macduff's flight, Macbeth resolves to kill every member of Macduff's family he can catch.*

---

### 1 'The Witches dance' (in small groups)

What kind of dance did the Witches perform for Macbeth? Create a suitable dance sequence, adding any language you think appropriate (for example, some of their lines).

### 2 Written for King James?

Some scholars think that lines 130–1 were spoken by the Witches to King James himself at a production in 1606.

### 3 'Dread exploits' (in pairs)

Macbeth resolves simply to follow his first instincts. A terrible massacre of innocent women and children will follow. Speak lines 143–54 ('Time . . . sights') as:

- a private, whispered thought
- a political broadcast to a huge audience
- the words of a very fearful man
- the words of an angry tyrant
- some other way.

Afterwards, talk together about how the lines should be spoken and what they add to your view of Macbeth. What kind of man has he become?

### 4 Are first thoughts best?

'The very firstlings of my heart shall be / The firstlings of my hand', says Macbeth. But are first thoughts best? Think about times when you have acted on first impulses, and whether you now feel that it would have been best to think things over carefully before acting.

---

**antic round** mad dance
**aye accursèd** cursed for ever
**flighty purpose** flying thoughts,
  first intentions

**trace him in his line** descend from
  him

FIRST WITCH  Ay, sir, all this is so. But why
          Stands Macbeth thus amazedly?            125
          Come, sisters, cheer we up his sprites,
          And show the best of our delights.
          I'll charm the air to give a sound,
          While you perform your antic round
          That this great king may kindly say,    130
          Our duties did his welcome pay.
            *Music. The Witches dance, and vanish*
MACBETH  Where are they? Gone? Let this pernicious hour,
          Stand aye accursèd in the calendar.
          Come in, without there!

              *Enter* LENNOX

LENNOX                    What's your grace's will?
MACBETH  Saw you the weïrd sisters?
LENNOX                  No, my lord.     135
MACBETH  Came they not by you?
LENNOX                No indeed, my lord.
MACBETH  Infected be the air whereon they ride,
          And damned all those that trust them. I did hear
          The galloping of horse. Who was't came by?
LENNOX  'Tis two or three, my lord, that bring you word   140
          Macduff is fled to England.
MACBETH               Fled to England?
LENNOX  Ay, my good lord.
MACBETH  [*Aside*] Time, thou anticipat'st my dread exploits;
          The flighty purpose never is o'ertook
          Unless the deed go with it. From this moment,   145
          The very firstlings of my heart shall be
          The firstlings of my hand. And even now
          To crown my thoughts with acts, be it thought and done.
          The castle of Macduff I will surprise;
          Seize upon Fife; give to th'edge o'th'sword   150
          His wife, his babes, and all unfortunate souls
          That trace him in his line. No boasting like a fool;
          This deed I'll do before this purpose cool,
          But no more sights. – Where are these gentlemen?
          Come, bring me where they are.     155
                     *Exeunt*

*Macduff's wife interprets his flight to England as madness, fear, or lack of love for his family. Ross comforts her: Macduff knows best, and even though the times are dangerous, they will improve.*

### 1 Husbands know best? (in pairs)

Why has Macduff left his family behind? Improvise the conversation between Macduff and his wife when he tells her he is going to England alone, leaving her in Scotland, even though the times are very dangerous. Use lines 2–14 as a basis for Lady Macduff's arguments.

### 2 Seeds of hope? (in groups of four or five)

Ross talks of the cruel times of Macbeth's tyranny. Men can be traitors without even knowing it themselves (lines 18–19); fears breed rumours (lines 19–20); and everyone is adrift in an unpredictable world (lines 21–2). But he thinks the tide will turn: evil will give way to good (lines 24–5).

Do you think his words reassure Lady Macduff? Talk together about whether you agree with Ross's view that bad always gives way to good.

### 3 Crocodile tears? (in groups of three or four)

Ross leaves, near to tears. In Roman Polanski's 1972 film of *Macbeth*, Ross is an obvious hypocrite, a time-server, who puts on a friendly face only to ensure that he can keep in with whoever is in power. As he leaves Macduff's castle, he waves the murderers in to kill everyone inside.

How do you see Ross? Look back through all he has said so far in the play and talk together about whether you think he is sincere, or just out for his own gain.

**titles** possessions
**wants the natural touch** lacks feeling for his family
**diminutive** tiny
**All is the fear . . . love** he's filled with fear, not love

**coz** cousin
**school** control
**the fits o'th'season** the violence of the times

# ACT 4   SCENE 2
## Fife   The castle of Macduff

*Enter* LADY MACDUFF, *her* SON, *and* ROSS

LADY MACDUFF  What had he done, to make him fly the land?
ROSS  You must have patience, madam.
LADY MACDUFF                    He had none;
    His flight was madness. When our actions do not,
    Our fears do make us traitors.
ROSS                              You know not
    Whether it was his wisdom or his fear.                         5
LADY MACDUFF  Wisdom? To leave his wife, to leave his babes,
    His mansion, and his titles in a place
    From whence himself does fly? He loves us not.
    He wants the natural touch, for the poor wren,
    The most diminutive of birds, will fight,                      10
    Her young ones in her nest, against the owl.
    All is the fear, and nothing is the love;
    As little is the wisdom, where the flight
    So runs against all reason.
ROSS                             My dearest coz,
    I pray you school yourself. But for your husband,             15
    He is noble, wise, judicious, and best knows
    The fits o'th'season. I dare not speak much further,
    But cruel are the times when we are traitors
    And do not know ourselves, when we hold rumour
    From what we fear, yet know not what we fear,                  20
    But float upon a wild and violent sea,
    Each way and none. I take my leave of you,
    Shall not be long but I'll be here again.
    Things at the worst will cease, or else climb upward
    To what they were before. My pretty cousin,                   25
    Blessing upon you.
LADY MACDUFF  Fathered he is, and yet he's fatherless.
ROSS  I am so much a fool, should I stay longer
    It would be my disgrace and your discomfort.
    I take my leave at once.                          *Exit*

*Macduff's son teases his mother affectionately. Behind his playful words are glimpses of the dangerous times: traps for the innocent, and widespread treachery. A messenger arrives to warn of danger.*

Lady Macduff and her son. Contrast this picture with those of Lady Macbeth on pages 37, 76, 132 and 134. If the two women had met earlier in the play, what might they have said to each other about loyalty, government, their husbands and the state of Scotland? Write or improvise such a scene.

**Sirrah** affectionate use of 'sir'
**lime/pitfall/gin** methods of catching birds: a glue-like paste smeared on trees/a pit/a trap to catch a bird by the head or legs

**swears** promises to tell the truth
**prattler** chatterbox
**in your state . . . perfect** I have only good intentions towards you

LADY MACDUFF                    Sirrah, your father's dead,    30
    And what will you do now? How will you live?
SON  As birds do, mother.
LADY MACDUFF          What, with worms and flies?
SON  With what I get I mean, and so do they.
LADY MACDUFF  Poor bird, thou'dst never fear the net, nor lime,
    the pitfall, nor the gin.    35
SON  Why should I, mother? Poor birds they are not set for.
    My father is not dead for all your saying.
LADY MACDUFF  Yes, he is dead. How wilt thou do for a father?
SON  Nay, how will you do for a husband?
LADY MACDUFF  Why, I can buy me twenty at any market.    40
SON  Then you'll buy 'em to sell again.
LADY MACDUFF  Thou speak'st with all thy wit, and yet i'faith
    with wit enough for thee.
SON  Was my father a traitor, mother?
LADY MACDUFF  Ay, that he was.    45
SON  What is a traitor?
LADY MACDUFF  Why, one that swears and lies.
SON  And be all traitors, that do so?
LADY MACDUFF  Every one that does so is a traitor and must be
    hanged.    50
SON  And must they all be hanged that swear and lie?
LADY MACDUFF  Every one.
SON  Who must hang them?
LADY MACDUFF  Why, the honest men.
SON  Then the liars and swearers are fools, for there are liars and    55
    swearers enough to beat the honest men and hang up them.
LADY MACDUFF  Now God help thee, poor monkey, but how wilt
    thou do for a father?
SON  If he were dead, you'd weep for him; if you would not, it were
    a good sign that I should quickly have a new father.    60
LADY MACDUFF  Poor prattler, how thou talk'st!

*Enter a* MESSENGER

MESSENGER  Bless you, fair dame. I am not to you known,
    Though in your state of honour I am perfect;
    I doubt some danger does approach you nearly.

*The messenger warns Lady Macduff to flee with her children because terrible danger is near. The Murderers enter, seeking Macduff. They kill his son and pursue Macduff's wife to murder her off stage.*

### 1 Who is the messenger? (in small groups)

Despite Macbeth's reign of terror, the messenger is willing to risk his life to warn the Macduffs. Every production must decide whether the messenger is an unknown person or someone who has already appeared in the play. In one production he was Macbeth himself, a touch which heightened the sense of his cruelty.

Talk together about the identity of the messenger. Then make up his or her own story which explains the warning visit to the Macduffs in spite of all the dangers.

### 2 Willing murderers (in pairs)

Once again, Macbeth has someone doing his dirty work for him. What kind of people are willing to undertake such dreadful business as murdering innocent women and children? What kind of society produces such callous killers? Talk together about what makes men willing to commit such appalling brutality in the service of a tyrant. Present your findings to the rest of the class.

### 3 On stage/off stage

In Greek tragedy, all killings take place off stage. The audience did not see the act of violence, but heard it reported later. Imagine that Shakespeare decided to copy the Greeks. Rewrite the last section of the scene as reported by a character in the play.

---

**homely** friendly
**fell cruelty** deadly danger
**Which is . . . person** which is close at hand
**laudable** praiseworthy

**unsanctified** unholy
**fry** young fish (notice how images of fertility are used as terms of abuse: 'egg' and 'fry')

If you will take a homely man's advice,                                    65
Be not found here. Hence with your little ones.
To fright you thus, methinks I am too savage;
To do worse to you were fell cruelty,
Which is too nigh your person. Heaven preserve you,
I dare abide no longer.                                    *Exit*
LADY MACDUFF                    Whither should I fly?        70
I have done no harm. But I remember now
I am in this earthly world where to do harm
Is often laudable, to do good sometime
Accounted dangerous folly. Why then, alas,
Do I put up that womanly defence,                          75
To say I have done no harm?

                    *Enter* MURDERERS

                         What are these faces?
A MURDERER Where is your husband?
LADY MACDUFF I hope in no place so unsanctified,
     Where such as thou mayst find him.
A MURDERER                         He's a traitor.
SON Thou liest, thou shag-haired villain.
A MURDERER                    What, you egg!            80
     Young fry of treachery!
                    [*Kills him*]
SON                         He has killed me, mother,
     Run away, I pray you!
               *Exit* [*Lady Macduff*] *crying 'Murder'*[, *pursued by*
                         *Murderers with her Son*]

Macbeth

*Macduff urges Malcolm to go to the defence of Scotland, which is suffering under Macbeth's tyranny. Malcolm voices his suspicions that Macduff has good reasons to betray him to Macbeth.*

---

## 1 England: design the scene (in pairs)

Work out a simple but effective way of showing the audience that this scene takes place in England at the palace of King Edward.

## 2 Malcolm's suspicions about Macduff

Malcolm builds a strong case for his mistrust of Macduff:

- he is not sure that Macduff is telling the truth (line 11)
- Macbeth was once thought to be honest (lines 12–13)
- Macduff was a friend of Macbeth (line 13)
- Macbeth has left Macduff unharmed (line 14)
- Macduff may betray Malcolm to Macbeth (lines 14–15)
- Macduff may kill Malcolm for Macbeth (lines 16–17)
- Macbeth is a traitor (line 18)
- even a good man may obey a wicked king (lines 19–20)
- evil often tries to look like good (lines 21–3)
- Macduff has abruptly left his family behind in danger (lines 26–8)
- Malcolm has cause to be suspicious for his own safety (lines 29–30).

Imagine that you are Macduff. Answer Malcolm's suspicions point by point.

## 3 Christian echoes (in small groups)

There is a religious image in each of the three longer speeches opposite. Identify them, then talk together about how each of them could apply to Macbeth himself.

---

**desolate shade** remote place
**mortal** deadly
**Bestride our downfall birthdom**
 defend our suffering birthplace
**Like syllable of dolour** similar cry
 of grief
**redress** make better
**discern of** be rewarded by

**recoil/In an imperial charge**
 serve a royal command
**transpose** change
**the brightest** Lucifer (who fell
 from God's grace)
**the brows of grace** the look of
 goodness

# ACT 4  SCENE 3
## England  The palace of King Edward

*Enter* MALCOLM *and* MACDUFF

MALCOLM  Let us seek out some desolate shade and there
    Weep our sad bosoms empty.
MACDUFF                      Let us rather
    Hold fast the mortal sword and like good men
    Bestride our downfall birthdom; each new morn,
    New widows howl, new orphans cry, new sorrows       5
    Strike heaven on the face, that it resounds
    As if it felt with Scotland and yelled out
    Like syllable of dolour.
MALCOLM                  What I believe, I'll wail;
    What know, believe; and what I can redress,
    As I shall find the time to friend, I will.           10
    What you have spoke, it may be so perchance.
    This tyrant, whose sole name blisters our tongues,
    Was once thought honest; you have loved him well –
    He hath not touched you yet. I am young, but something
    You may discern of him through me, and wisdom      15
    To offer up a weak, poor, innocent lamb
    T'appease an angry god.
MACDUFF  I am not treacherous.
MALCOLM                But Macbeth is.
    A good and virtuous nature may recoil
    In an imperial charge. But I shall crave your pardon:     20
    That which you are, my thoughts cannot transpose;
    Angels are bright still, though the brightest fell.
    Though all things foul would wear the brows of grace,
    Yet grace must still look so.
MACDUFF              I have lost my hopes.
MALCOLM  Perchance even there where I did find my doubts.     25
    Why in that rawness left you wife and child,
    Those precious motives, those strong knots of love,
    Without leave-taking? I pray you,

*Malcolm's suspicions dismay Macduff. Malcolm tells him that he has
English troops to support his cause, but that his own vices are far
worse than Macbeth's.*

### 1 A suspicious visitor (in pairs)

Malcolm is elaborately testing Macduff's sincerity. The terror of
Macbeth's regime has made him fearful of visitors; after all, they may
be Macbeth's secret agents.

Improvise a situation in which one person is an exile, under
sentence of death, from a police state. An old friend from that country
comes to visit. How can you be sure they are genuine?

A historical parallel that shows
Malcolm has good reasons for his
fears. Leon Trotsky (right) was
Stalin's friend and ally in the
Russian Revolution of 1917, but he
fled Russia to escape Stalin's
tyranny. One of Stalin's agents
tricked his way into Trotsky's
confidence at his safe haven in
Mexico, then assassinated him with
an ice-pick. Tyrants never forgive or
forget.

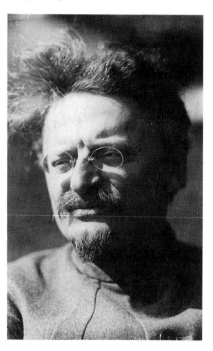

| | |
|---|---|
| **jealousies** suspicions | **withal** besides |
| **lay thou thy basis sure** rest secure | **hands uplifted in my right** |
| **affeered** confirmed (that is to say, | soldiers supporting me |
| Macbeth is securely king) | **grafted** rooted, ingrained |
| **to boot** as well | **be opened** come to flower |
| **the yoke** slavery | **confineless harms** limitless evils |

  Let not my jealousies be your dishonours,
  But mine own safeties; you may be rightly just,       30
  Whatever I shall think.
MACDUFF          Bleed, bleed, poor country.
  Great tyranny, lay thou thy basis sure,
  For goodness dare not check thee; wear thou thy wrongs,
  The title is affeered. Fare thee well, lord,
  I would not be the villain that thou think'st      35
  For the whole space that's in the tyrant's grasp,
  And the rich East to boot.
MALCOLM         Be not offended.
  I speak not as in absolute fear of you:
  I think our country sinks beneath the yoke;
  It weeps, it bleeds, and each new day a gash      40
  Is added to her wounds. I think withal
  There would be hands uplifted in my right,
  And here from gracious England have I offer
  Of goodly thousands. But for all this,
  When I shall tread upon the tyrant's head,       45
  Or wear it on my sword, yet my poor country
  Shall have more vices than it had before,
  More suffer, and more sundry ways than ever,
  By him that shall succeed.
MACDUFF         What should he be?
MALCOLM  It is myself I mean – in whom I know      50
  All the particulars of vice so grafted
  That when they shall be opened, black Macbeth
  Will seem as pure as snow, and the poor state
  Esteem him as a lamb, being compared
  With my confineless harms.
MACDUFF         Not in the legions    55
  Of horrid hell can come a devil more damned
  In evils to top Macbeth.

*Malcolm lists Macbeth's vices, but claims that his own sexual desire is limitless, and he is infinitely greedy. Macduff finds reasons to excuse Malcolm's ungovernable lust and greed.*

## 1 Macbeth's evil (in groups of six to ten)

Malcolm names eight of Macbeth's evils (lines 57–60). He is 'bloody' (murderous), 'luxurious' (lecherous), 'avaricious' (greedy), 'false', 'deceitful', 'sudden' (violent), 'malicious', and possesses 'every sin that has a name' (the seven deadly sins).

Work out a sequence of eight tableaux or short mimes to show Macbeth's nature. Each scene will show a quality mentioned in lines 57–60. Add a commentary to your presentation if you wish.

## 2 A man's view of women (in groups of four)

Macduff doesn't find many problems with Malcolm's limitless lecherousness. 'We have willing dames enough', he says, claiming that there will be more women than even Malcolm can cope with who will be willing to prostitute themselves to a king ('to greatness dedicate themselves').

Talk together about Macduff's dismissal of lust as an unimportant quality in a leader. Is that the kind of thing only a man could say? Use examples of the much-publicised sexual activities of contemporary politicians as evidence in your arguments.

## 3 Greed – now that's more serious! (in groups of four)

Greed is much more serious than excessive sexual appetite, says Macduff (lines 84–7). But even that doesn't really count against a leader! Discuss what you think of Macduff's reasoning. What does it suggest to you about his views of a good ruler?

---

**voluptuousness** lust
**continent impediments** restraints
**Boundless intemperance** limitless lust
**Convey your pleasures** have sex
**hoodwink** deceive

**ill-composed affection** wicked emotions
**stanchless avarice** unquenchable greed
**foisons** plenty, abundance
**your mere own** simply of your own
**portable** bearable

MALCOLM                    I grant him bloody,
    Luxurious, avaricious, false, deceitful,
    Sudden, malicious, smacking of every sin
    That has a name. But there's no bottom, none,    60
    In my voluptuousness: your wives, your daughters,
    Your matrons, and your maids could not fill up
    The cistern of my lust, and my desire
    All continent impediments would o'erbear
    That did oppose my will. Better Macbeth,    65
    Than such an one to reign.
MACDUFF                    Boundless intemperance
    In nature is a tyranny; it hath been
    Th'untimely emptying of the happy throne
    And fall of many kings. But fear not yet
    To take upon you what is yours: you may    70
    Convey your pleasures in a spacious plenty
    And yet seem cold. The time you may so hoodwink.
    We have willing dames enough; there cannot be
    That vulture in you to devour so many
    As will to greatness dedicate themselves,    75
    Finding it so inclined.
MALCOLM                    With this, there grows
    In my most ill-composed affection such
    A stanchless avarice that, were I king,
    I should cut off the nobles for their lands,
    Desire his jewels, and this other's house,    80
    And my more-having would be as a sauce
    To make me hunger more, that I should forge
    Quarrels unjust against the good and loyal,
    Destroying them for wealth.
MACDUFF                    This avarice
    Sticks deeper, grows with more pernicious root    85
    Than summer-seeming lust, and it hath been
    The sword of our slain kings; yet do not fear,
    Scotland hath foisons to fill up your will
    Of your mere own. All these are portable,
    With other graces weighed.    90

*Malcolm claims that he has no good qualities whatsoever, and seeks only to create chaos. Macduff condemns Malcolm as unfit to rule. Malcolm says that Macduff's reaction has removed his suspicions. He denies all vices.*

### 1 The good king (in groups of six to twelve)

In lines 92–4 Malcolm lists twelve qualities that a good king should possess: 'justice' (fairness), 'verity' (truthfulness), 'temp'rance' (self-control), 'stableness' (even-temperedness), 'bounty' (generosity), 'perseverance' (endurance), 'mercy' (forgiveness), 'lowliness' (humility), 'devotion' (piety), 'patience', 'courage', 'fortitude' (strength).

Work out a way of showing 'the king-becoming graces' (for example, a sequence of tableaux or mimes).

### 2 Who's who? (in pairs)

Macduff's impassioned outburst in lines 102–14 includes references to Malcolm, Macbeth, Duncan, Duncan's wife, Scotland and Macduff himself. As one person reads a line at a time, the other identifies aloud to whom (or what) Macduff is referring (for example, in line 102 it's 'Malcolm', in line 103 'Malcolm' and 'Scotland').

### 3 What's Malcolm really like?

In lines 125–31, Malcolm says what he's really like. Make a list of the qualities he describes (the punctuation will help you). Then compare the list with the qualities of kingship in lines 92–4. What characteristics has Malcolm not mentioned – and why? What's your view of his character?

---

**division** variety
**concord** peace
**truest issue** legitimate heir
  (Malcolm)
**interdiction** condemnation
**blaspheme his breed** slander his
  family
**upon her knees** praying

**scruples** suspicions
**trains** tricks
**modest wisdom . . . over-
  credulous haste** common sense
  saved me
**detraction** accusations
**abjure** reject
**forsworn** untruthful

MALCOLM  But I have none. The king-becoming graces –
　　　　　As justice, verity, temp'rance, stableness,
　　　　　Bounty, perseverance, mercy, lowliness,
　　　　　Devotion, patience, courage, fortitude –
　　　　　I have no relish of them, but abound　　　　　　　　95
　　　　　In the division of each several crime,
　　　　　Acting it many ways. Nay, had I power, I should
　　　　　Pour the sweet milk of concord into hell,
　　　　　Uproar the universal peace, confound
　　　　　All unity on earth.
MACDUFF　　　　　　　　O Scotland, Scotland!　　　　100
MALCOLM  If such a one be fit to govern, speak.
　　　　　I am as I have spoken.
MACDUFF　　　　　　　　Fit to govern?
　　　　　No, not to live. O nation miserable!
　　　　　With an untitled tyrant, bloody-sceptred,
　　　　　When shalt thou see thy wholesome days again,　　105
　　　　　Since that the truest issue of thy throne
　　　　　By his own interdiction stands accursed
　　　　　And does blaspheme his breed? Thy royal father
　　　　　Was a most sainted king; the queen that bore thee,
　　　　　Oft'ner upon her knees than on her feet,　　　　110
　　　　　Died every day she lived. Fare thee well,
　　　　　These evils thou repeat'st upon thyself
　　　　　Hath banished me from Scotland. O my breast,
　　　　　Thy hope ends here.
MALCOLM　　　　　　　　Macduff, this noble passion,
　　　　　Child of integrity, hath from my soul　　　　　115
　　　　　Wiped the black scruples, reconciled my thoughts
　　　　　To thy good truth and honour. Devilish Macbeth
　　　　　By many of these trains hath sought to win me
　　　　　Into his power, and modest wisdom plucks me
　　　　　From over-credulous haste; but God above　　　120
　　　　　Deal between thee and me, for even now
　　　　　I put myself to thy direction and
　　　　　Unspeak mine own detraction, here abjure
　　　　　The taints and blames I laid upon myself,
　　　　　For strangers to my nature. I am yet　　　　　125
　　　　　Unknown to woman, never was forsworn,

*Malcolm asserts his virtue and declares he is now ready to invade Scotland.*
*The Doctor tells how King Edward cures sick people by his touch. Malcolm*
*says the gift of healing is passed down to future kings.*

### 1 'Why are you silent?'

What is Macduff thinking at this moment (line 137) after Malcolm
has just revealed that he's only been testing him?

### 2 Curing the sick (in groups of six to eight)

'The Evil' (or King's Evil) was scrofula, a type of tuberculosis. It was
thought that the 'strangely visited' (very sick people) could be cured
by the touch of the king, who would then hang a 'stamp' (coin or
medal) round their neck. The practice of 'touching' continued until
the late eighteenth century.

Prepare a presentation of the ceremony described in lines 149–56.
End your ceremony with a prophecy spoken by the king (line 159)
about Malcolm and Macbeth.

### 3 The good king

Some critics argue that the Doctor's lines were inserted to flatter
King James I, but there are other reasons for them. How does the
description of the benign powers of King Edward add to your
understanding of *Macbeth*? Think of ways in which the Doctor's lines
about the life-healing powers of the English king add dramatic and
symbolic significance to the play.

---

**coveted** desired
**here-approach** arrival here
**at a point** prepared for war
**stay his cure** await his healing
 touch

**their malady . . . art** illnesses
 defeat the efforts of medical
 science
**sanctity** holiness
**here-remain** stay
**solicits** entreats
**benediction** blessing

Scarcely have coveted what was mine own,
At no time broke my faith, would not betray
The devil to his fellow, and delight
No less in truth than life. My first false speaking          130
Was this upon myself. What I am truly
Is thine and my poor country's to command:
Whither indeed, before thy here-approach,
Old Siward with ten thousand warlike men
Already at a point was setting forth.          135
Now we'll together, and the chance of goodness
Be like our warranted quarrel. Why are you silent?
MACDUFF  Such welcome and unwelcome things at once,
'Tis hard to reconcile.

*Enter a* DOCTOR

MALCOLM                              Well, more anon. –
Comes the king forth, I pray you?          140
DOCTOR  Ay, sir: there are a crew of wretched souls
That stay his cure; their malady convinces
The great assay of art, but at his touch,
Such sanctity hath heaven given his hand,
They presently amend.                              *Exit*  145
MALCOLM  I thank you, doctor.
MACDUFF  What's the disease he means?
MALCOLM  'Tis called the Evil.
A most miraculous work in this good king,
Which often since my here-remain in England          150
I have seen him do. How he solicits heaven
Himself best knows, but strangely visited people
All swoll'n and ulcerous, pitiful to the eye,
The mere despair of surgery, he cures,
Hanging a golden stamp about their necks          155
Put on with holy prayers, and 'tis spoken
To the succeeding royalty he leaves
The healing benediction. With this strange virtue,
He hath a heavenly gift of prophecy,
And sundry blessings hang about his throne          160
That speak him full of grace.

*Enter* ROSS

MACDUFF                              See who comes here.

*Ross reports that in Scotland suffering goes unremarked and good men's lives are short. He says that Macduff's family is well. Rebellion against Macbeth is rumoured. Malcolm reveals his plan to invade Scotland.*

## 1 Bringing bad news (in small groups)

Ross knows what's happened to Macduff's family. Why doesn't he immediately tell his terrible news? Talk together about why you think Ross delays in telling Macduff the news of the murder of his family.

Imagine that you have some very bad news to break to a friend. How will you do it?

## 2 A journey to England

Write Ross's diary entries as he travels from Scotland to England. Report what he sees (lines 166–75 and 183–7) and his thoughts about the terrible news he has for Macduff.

## 3 Pacing the scene

Every theatre director attempts to vary the pace at which the words are spoken, and to ensure that each word is appropriately emphasised. Work carefully through the page opposite and write notes on the pace and tone of each speech. Identify any words you think should be given special emphasis. Remember that pauses can often have as great a significance in theatre productions as the spoken word itself. Suggest where pauses could be made to intensify dramatic effect.

**betimes** swiftly
**not marked** go unnoticed
**A modern ecstasy** everyday feeling
**knell** death bell
**relation/Too nice** too accurate a story

**doth hiss the speaker** is just stale news
**teems** gives birth to
**niggard** miser
**out** in rebellion
**afoot** marching
**eye** presence
**doff** remove

MALCOLM  My countryman, but yet I know him not.
MACDUFF  My ever gentle cousin, welcome hither.
MALCOLM  I know him now. Good God betimes remove
   The means that makes us strangers.
ROSS         Sir, amen.    165
MACDUFF  Stands Scotland where it did?
ROSS        Alas, poor country,
   Almost afraid to know itself. It cannot
   Be called our mother, but our grave, where nothing
   But who knows nothing is once seen to smile;
   Where sighs, and groans, and shrieks that rend the air  170
   Are made, not marked; where violent sorrow seems
   A modern ecstasy. The deadman's knell
   Is there scarce asked for who, and good men's lives
   Expire before the flowers in their caps,
   Dying or ere they sicken.
MACDUFF      O relation    175
   Too nice, and yet too true.
MALCOLM     What's the newest grief?
ROSS  That of an hour's age doth hiss the speaker;
   Each minute teems a new one.
MACDUFF      How does my wife?
ROSS  Why, well.
MACDUFF  And all my children?
ROSS      Well, too.
MACDUFF  The tyrant has not battered at their peace?  180
ROSS  No, they were well at peace when I did leave 'em.
MACDUFF  Be not a niggard of your speech: how goes't?
ROSS  When I came hither to transport the tidings
   Which I have heavily borne, there ran a rumour
   Of many worthy fellows that were out,    185
   Which was to my belief witnessed the rather
   For that I saw the tyrant's power afoot.
   Now is the time of help. [*To Malcolm*] Your eye in
    Scotland
   Would create soldiers, make our women fight
   To doff their dire distresses.
MALCOLM     Be't their comfort  190
   We are coming thither. Gracious England hath
   Lent us good Siward and ten thousand men –

*Ross tells of the murder of Macduff's family. Malcolm tries to comfort Macduff, who struggles with his grief over the slaughter of his wife and children.*

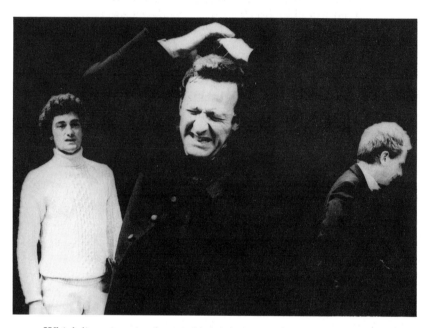

Which line opposite do you think is being spoken at this moment?

## 1 Telling bad news (in groups of three)

How does Ross deliver his terrible news to Macduff? In the theatre, there is a convention that, when a line is shared between two speakers, there is no pause. One character speaks immediately after the other.

Take parts and read lines 194–221 first without pauses, and then with pauses. Which style seems the most appropriate?

| | |
|---|---|
| **latch** catch | **o'erfraught** overburdened |
| **The general cause** everyone | **hell-kite** bird of prey from Hell |
| **fee-grief** personal sorrow | **dam** mother |
| **quarry** heap of slaughtered animals | **fell swoop** deadly attack |

An older and a better soldier none
That Christendom gives out.
ROSS                              Would I could answer
This comfort with the like. But I have words                    195
That would be howled out in the desert air,
Where hearing should not latch them.
MACDUFF                              What concern they?
The general cause, or is it a fee-grief
Due to some single breast?
ROSS                              No mind that's honest
But in it shares some woe, though the main part                200
Pertains to you alone.
MACDUFF               If it be mine,
Keep it not from me; quickly let me have it.
ROSS  Let not your ears despise my tongue forever
Which shall possess them with the heaviest sound
That ever yet they heard.
MACDUFF               H'm – I guess at it.                      205
ROSS  Your castle is surprised; your wife and babes
Savagely slaughtered. To relate the manner
Were on the quarry of these murdered deer
To add the death of you.
MALCOLM               Merciful heaven –
What, man, ne'er pull your hat upon your brows:                210
Give sorrow words; the grief that does not speak,
Whispers the o'erfraught heart and bids it break.
MACDUFF  My children too?
ROSS                         Wife, children, servants, all
That could be found.
MACDUFF               And I must be from thence?
My wife killed too?
ROSS                  I have said.
MALCOLM               Be comforted.                            215
Let's make us med'cines of our great revenge
To cure this deadly grief.
MACDUFF  He has no children. All my pretty ones?
Did you say all? O hell-kite! All?
What, all my pretty chickens and their dam                     220
At one fell swoop?

*Macduff cannot hide his grief. He feels that he is to blame for his family's death. He vows vengeance on Macbeth. Malcolm declares that the time is ripe to overthrow Macbeth, as Heaven itself is against him.*

### 1 What is a man? (in pairs)

Earlier in the play, Lady Macbeth has taunted Macbeth for not behaving like 'a man'. Now Malcolm (lines 222 and 238) and Macduff (line 224) show different interpretations of what it is to be a man. Talk together about what Malcolm and Macduff have in mind as they speak.

### 2 Malcolm writes to his brother

Write the letter to Donaldbain in Ireland which Malcolm sends immediately after this scene.

### 3 Would you cut the scene? (in groups of eight or more)

Some productions of *Macbeth* do not present Act 4 Scene 3 on stage at all. Imagine that you are about to put on the play. Split your group equally in half. One side argues that the scene should be cut entirely; the others argue for keeping it in your production. Listen carefully to your opponents' reasons to cut or not to cut, and try to answer them.

### 4 The longest scene (in small groups)

Act 4 Scene 3 is the longest scene in the play. Explore ways of presenting it in the briefest time, but including all its major elements.

---

**Naught** wicked
**demerits** faults
**whetstone** sharpening stone
**braggart** boaster
**intermission** interval of time
**Front to front** face to face

**our lack . . . leave** we have only to make our farewells
**powers above** angels
**instruments** trumpets (or weapons, or soldiers)

MALCOLM  Dispute it like a man.
MACDUFF  I shall do so;
   But I must also feel it as a man;
   I cannot but remember such things were    225
   That were most precious to me. Did heaven look on,
   And would not take their part? Sinful Macduff,
   They were all struck for thee. Naught that I am,
   Not for their own demerits but for mine,
   Fell slaughter on their souls. Heaven rest them now.  230
MALCOLM  Be this the whetstone of your sword, let grief
   Convert to anger. Blunt not the heart, enrage it.
MACDUFF  O, I could play the woman with mine eyes
   And braggart with my tongue. But gentle heavens,
   Cut short all intermission. Front to front    235
   Bring thou this fiend of Scotland and myself;
   Within my sword's length set him. If he scape,
   Heaven forgive him too.
MALCOLM       This tune goes manly.
   Come, go we to the king; our power is ready;
   Our lack is nothing but our leave. Macbeth   240
   Is ripe for shaking, and the powers above
   Put on their instruments. Receive what cheer you may:
   The night is long that never finds the day.
               *Exeunt*

# Looking back at Act 4
*Activities for groups or individuals*

### 1 Macbeth's tricks (in pairs)

In Scene 3 Malcolm says that Macbeth has already tried to tempt him with offers of women, money and other incentives (lines 117–20). Write a letter from Macbeth tempting Malcolm back to Scotland.

### 2 Is Malcolm a political schemer?

What kind of man is Malcolm? Often he is played as a person of great integrity, who will become a truly noble future king. But some productions present him as devious: a political schemer, lacking truthfulness and goodwill, who will become yet another brutal war-lord. Experiment with different ways of reading Malcolm's lines in Scene 3 as he 'tests' Macduff. Then write your own assessment of his character.

### 3 'How many children had Lady Macbeth?'

'He has no children', cries Macduff in Scene 3 as he is advised to seek revenge on Macbeth. But in Act 1 Scene 7 Lady Macbeth says that she has suckled a child at her breast. Millions of words have been written on the question: did she have children? Some theatre productions of *Macbeth* make 'children' a central concept. The historical Lady Macbeth had one child by her first husband, but none by Macbeth. But does it matter, in the play, whether she has children or not?

### 4 Three: a magic number

Three was supposed to be a magic number, favoured by witches. Look back through Scene 1 to discover how many examples you can find of things happening, or being said, in threes.

### 5 What is a traitor?

Whether someone is 'a traitor' or 'a freedom-fighter' depends on who is using the label. To Macbeth, Macduff is a traitor, but is he a traitor in your eyes?

## 6 Different views of the Witches

**a** A woodcut of 1619 showing three Witches with their familiars.
**b** The Witches in a 1938 production at Stratford-upon-Avon.
**c** A 1992 Berlin production of *Macbeth*.

Do any of these match your impressions of the Witches? How would you present them?

*The Gentlewoman reports to the Doctor that she has seen Lady Macbeth sleepwalking. She refuses to tell what her mistress has said in her sleep. Lady Macbeth, asleep, enters with a candle.*

## 1 Staging the scene (in groups of four to six)

This is one of the most famous scenes in world drama. Work out how you would stage it to maximum dramatic effect by preparing notes for your actors. Then act it!

## 2 What did Lady Macbeth write?

The Gentlewoman tells how she has seen Lady Macbeth carefully take paper, fold it, write on it, read it, and seal it – all in her sleep. What did Lady Macbeth write? A letter to Macbeth? A confession? Her will? A warning to Lady Macduff? Or . . . ? Write Lady Macbeth's document.

'Yet here's a spot.' Lady Macbeth in a Taiwanese adaptation, *The Kingdom of Desire*.

| | |
|---|---|
| **the field** the battlefield | **meet** fitting |
| **closet** chest for valuables | ***taper*** candle |
| **perturbation** disturbance | **guise** custom |
| **watching** waking | **seem** appear to be |
| **slumbery agitation** sleepwalking | |

# ACT 5   SCENE 1
## A room in Dunsinane Castle

*Enter a* DOCTOR *of physic, and a* WAITING-GENTLEWOMAN

DOCTOR I have two nights watched with you, but can perceive no
truth in your report. When was it she last walked?

GENTLEWOMAN Since his majesty went into the field, I have seen
her rise from her bed, throw her night-gown upon her, unlock
her closet, take forth paper, fold it, write upon't, read it, after- 5
wards seal it, and again return to bed, yet all this while in a
most fast sleep.

DOCTOR A great perturbation in nature, to receive at once the
benefit of sleep and do the effects of watching. In this slumbery
agitation, besides her walking and other actual performances, 10
what at any time have you heard her say?

GENTLEWOMAN That, sir, which I will not report after her.

DOCTOR You may to me, and 'tis most meet you should.

GENTLEWOMAN Neither to you, nor anyone, having no witness to
confirm my speech. 15

*Enter* LADY [MACBETH], *with a taper*

Lo you, here she comes. This is her very guise and, upon my
life, fast asleep. Observe her, stand close.

DOCTOR How came she by that light?

GENTLEWOMAN Why, it stood by her. She has light by her con-
tinually, 'tis her command. 20

DOCTOR You see her eyes are open.

GENTLEWOMAN Ay, but their sense are shut.

DOCTOR What is it she does now? Look how she rubs her hands.

GENTLEWOMAN It is an accustomed action with her, to seem thus
washing her hands; I have known her continue in this a quarter 25
of an hour.

LADY MACBETH Yet here's a spot.

DOCTOR Hark, she speaks; I will set down what comes from her to
satisfy my remembrance the more strongly.

*Lady Macbeth, fast asleep, tries to wash imagined blood from her hands. Her fragmented language echoes her own and Macbeth's words about past murders: Duncan, Lady Macduff, Banquo.*

## 1 Dream – or nightmare?
(in groups of six to eight)

Lady Macbeth's tortured imagination roams over her past conversations with her husband. Present her dream (lines 30–58) as vividly as you can. Here are two possibilities:

a Accompany everything she says with a mime of her actions, or the pictures she sees in her mind.

b Add echoes. Look back at her previous appearances in the play. Select lines that echo what she says in her sleepwalking (for example, 'A little water clears us of this deed'). Use the lines as a chorus of repetitive echoes as Lady Macbeth speaks.

**You mar all with this starting** you spoil everything with your nervousness
**sorely charged** heavily burdened
**the dignity of the whole body** the sake of life itself

**Foul whisp'rings are abroad** terrible rumours are circulating
**divine** priest
**mated** confused

LADY MACBETH Out damned spot! Out, I say! One, two. Why 30
then 'tis time to do't. Hell is murky. Fie, my lord, fie, a soldier,
and afeard? What need we fear? Who knows it, when none can
call our power to account? Yet who would have thought the old
man to have had so much blood in him?

DOCTOR Do you mark that? 35

LADY MACBETH The Thane of Fife had a wife. Where is she
now? What, will these hands ne'er be clean? No more o'that,
my lord, no more o'that. You mar all with this starting.

DOCTOR Go to, go to; you have known what you should not.

GENTLEWOMAN She has spoke what she should not, I am sure of 40
that. Heaven knows what she has known.

LADY MACBETH Here's the smell of the blood still; all the per-
fumes of Arabia will not sweeten this little hand. O, O, O.

DOCTOR What a sigh is there? The heart is sorely charged.

GENTLEWOMAN I would not have such a heart in my bosom for 45
the dignity of the whole body.

DOCTOR Well, well, well –

GENTLEWOMAN Pray God it be, sir.

DOCTOR This disease is beyond my practice; yet I have known
those which have walked in their sleep who have died holily in 50
their beds.

LADY MACBETH Wash your hands, put on your night-gown, look
not so pale. I tell you yet again, Banquo's buried; he cannot
come out on's grave.

DOCTOR Even so? 55

LADY MACBETH To bed, to bed; there's knocking at the gate.
Come, come, come, come, give me your hand; what's done
cannot be undone. To bed, to bed, to bed. *Exit*

DOCTOR Will she go now to bed?

GENTLEWOMAN Directly. 60

DOCTOR Foul whisp'rings are abroad; unnatural deeds
Do breed unnatural troubles; infected minds
To their deaf pillows will discharge their secrets.
More needs she the divine than the physician.
God, God forgive us all. Look after her; 65
Remove from her the means of all annoyance,
And still keep eyes upon her. So, good night,
My mind she has mated and amazed my sight.
I think, but dare not speak.

GENTLEWOMAN                    Good night, good doctor.
                                              *Exeunt*

*News! Malcolm, Macduff, Siward and the English army approach; young men flock to join them; Macbeth is troubled by internal revolt – his soldiers obey him only out of fear, and his conscience oppresses him.*

## 1 Hope! (in groups of four)

The four thanes are full of hope because of Macbeth's difficulties and the approach of Malcolm's army. They can see, not far ahead, freedom from tyranny. Read lines 1–31 in two ways:

First, in whispers, as conspirators. Take turns, reading only up to a punctuation mark, then hand on.

Second, take parts as the four thanes and read through the scene.

Which reading conveys most powerfully a sense of mounting optimism?

## 2 Views of Macbeth (in groups of three to six)

One person reads lines 12–25, describing Macbeth. Read a short section at a time. The others mime each description. Some sections are easy to present as actions, others will take longer to work out.

## 3 Clothing

Lines 15–16 and 20–2 use images of clothing to describe Macbeth. Imagine that you are a cartoonist on a Scottish newspaper. Your editor asks you to produce a cartoon of Macbeth using one or other of these images. Add a suitable caption.

## 4 The soldiers' views (in groups of three to five)

Ordinary people don't get much of a voice in this play. As a group of soldiers, standing near the thanes in this scene, improvise your conversation as you march towards Birnam.

---

**colours** flags, banners
**Excite the mortified man** bring the dead to life
**file** list
**unrough . . . manhood** unbearded young men, inexperienced in battle
**distempered cause** diseased regime

**Now minutely . . . faith-breach** every minute there's a rebellion protesting against his treachery
**the med'cine . . . weal** Malcolm (the cure of the diseased kingdom)
**purge** cure by cleansing

# ACT 5 SCENE 2
## Scotland Open country

Drum and colours. Enter MENTEITH, CAITHNESS, ANGUS,
LENNOX, soldiers

MENTEITH  The English power is near, led on by Malcolm,
His uncle Siward, and the good Macduff.
Revenges burn in them, for their dear causes
Would to the bleeding and the grim alarm
Excite the mortified man.

ANGUS                          Near Birnam Wood          5
Shall we well meet them; that way are they coming.

CAITHNESS  Who knows if Donaldbain be with his brother?

LENNOX  For certain, sir, he is not. I have a file
Of all the gentry; there is Siward's son
And many unrough youths that even now          10
Protest their first of manhood.

MENTEITH                          What does the tyrant?

CAITHNESS  Great Dunsinane he strongly fortifies.
Some say he's mad; others that lesser hate him
Do call it valiant fury, but for certain
He cannot buckle his distempered cause          15
Within the belt of rule.

ANGUS                          Now does he feel
His secret murders sticking on his hands.
Now minutely revolts upbraid his faith-breach;
Those he commands, move only in command,
Nothing in love. Now does he feel his title          20
Hang loose about him, like a giant's robe
Upon a dwarfish thief.

MENTEITH                          Who then shall blame
His pestered senses to recoil and start,
When all that is within him does condemn
Itself for being there?

CAITHNESS                          Well, march we on          25
To give obedience where 'tis truly owed;
Meet we the med'cine of the sickly weal,
And with him pour we in our country's purge,
Each drop of us.

*Macbeth, receiving news of desertions from his army, recalls the Witches'*
*predictions. He rages at the soldier who tells of Malcolm's approach.*
*He knows that the coming battle will make or break him.*

## 1 'No more reports'

Every military commander relies on intelligence (the reports he
receives about the enemy). Write several reports that Macbeth has
received from his agents.

## 2 Deserters (in groups of three to five)

'Let them fly all', cries Macbeth as he hears that more of his followers
have deserted him. Improvise a conversation between a group of
soldiers in Macbeth's army as they argue whether or not to desert.

## 3 'Thou cream-faced loon' (in pairs)

Lines 11–17 are rich in insults. Hurl them at each other! What does
the language tell you about the appearance of the unfortunate
servant?

## 4 Macbeth's mood (in pairs)

Macbeth's mood has been described in the previous scene as 'mad' or
'valiant fury'. To help you find Macbeth's mood and tone of voice,
speak all that he says in lines 1–61. One person starts with a short
section ('Bring me no more reports'). The partner speaks a following
short section ('let them fly all') and so on, in turns throughout the
scene. Speak only Macbeth's lines.

Afterwards, talk together about whether you think Macbeth uses
the same tone throughout, or whether there are sections where the
tone changes. Then prepare notes for an actor advising him how he
might speak throughout this scene.

---

**dew the sovereign flower** restore
  the rightful king
**taint** become infected, weaken
**mortal consequences** human
  destiny

**epicures** luxury-lovers
**sway by** rule, control
**cheer . . . disseat** comfort me or
  dethrone me

LENNOX                    Or so much as it needs
                To dew the sovereign flower and drown the weeds.            30
                Make we our march towards Birnam.

                                                *Exeunt, marching*


## ACT 5    SCENE 3
## Dunsinane Castle


*Enter* MACBETH, DOCTOR, *and attendants*

MACBETH  Bring me no more reports, let them fly all;
                Till Birnam Wood remove to Dunsinane,
                I cannot taint with fear. What's the boy Malcolm?
                Was he not born of woman? The spirits that know
                All mortal consequences have pronounced me thus:            5
                'Fear not, Macbeth, no man that's born of woman
                Shall e'er have power upon thee.' Then fly false thanes
                And mingle with the English epicures;
                The mind I sway by and the heart I bear
                Shall never sag with doubt nor shake with fear.            10

                        *Enter* SERVANT

                The devil damn thee black, thou cream-faced loon.
                Where got'st thou that goose-look?
SERVANT  There is ten thousand –
MACBETH                                Geese, villain?
SERVANT                                                Soldiers, sir.
MACBETH  Go prick thy face and over-red thy fear,
                Thou lily-livered boy. What soldiers, patch?            15
                Death of thy soul, those linen cheeks of thine
                Are counsellors to fear. What soldiers, whey-face?
SERVANT  The English force, so please you.
MACBETH  Take thy face hence!
                                                *[Exit Servant]*
                        Seyton! – I am sick at heart,
                When I behold – Seyton, I say! – this push            20
                Will cheer me ever or disseat me now.

*Macbeth reflects on a bleak future. He determines to fight to the death, and orders rumour-mongers to be killed. When the Doctor tells him that he cannot cure mental disorders, Macbeth dismisses medicine.*

## 1 Old age

Macbeth broods on his future in lines 22–8. He describes four things that old people hope for (line 25), and three that he's likely to receive (lines 27–8). Make up a sentence to illustrate each thing Macbeth mentions. Each sentence should begin: 'When I'm old, people will . . .'.

## 2 Seyton = Satan? (in groups of four)

In some productions of the play, Seyton is pronounced 'Satan' (King of Hell). Talk together about whether you think that adds to the drama. Decide how Seyton should behave and what he would wear.

## 3 Shakespeare as Sigmund Freud? (in pairs)

Three hundred years before Sigmund Freud, Shakespeare seems to have invented psychoanalysis. Macbeth's description of 'a mind diseased' (lines 41–6) exactly catches the anxiety, depression and sorrow that Freud sought to cure by psychoanalysis. Freud's method, in essence, is exactly what the Doctor states in lines 46–7: 'Therein the patient/Must minister to himself'. This states the heart of psychoanalytic practice: the patient, by talking through his or her problems with an analyst, effectively finds his or her own cure.

Psychoanalyse Lady Macbeth: one person as patient, one as psychoanalyst. The analyst asks questions to help Lady Macbeth find out what's troubling her.

---

sere withered
mouth-honour, breath lip service, flattery
fain gladly
skirr scour
thick-coming fancies frequent nightmares

minister to cure
Raze out the written troubles erase the deep anxieties
physic medicine
cast/The water analyse the urine
purge cure by cleansing
pristine original, fresh

I have lived long enough. My way of life
Is fall'n into the sere, the yellow leaf,
And that which should accompany old age,
As honour, love, obedience, troops of friends,                    25
I must not look to have; but in their stead,
Curses, not loud but deep, mouth-honour, breath
Which the poor heart would fain deny, and dare not.
Seyton!

*Enter* SEYTON

SEYTON  What's your gracious pleasure?
MACBETH                               What news more?          30
SEYTON  All is confirmed, my lord, which was reported.
MACBETH  I'll fight till from my bones my flesh be hacked.
        Give me my armour.
SEYTON  'Tis not needed yet.
MACBETH  I'll put it on;                                        35
        Send out more horses; skirr the country round.
        Hang those that talk of fear. Give me mine armour.
        How does your patient, doctor?
DOCTOR                               Not so sick, my lord,
        As she is troubled with thick-coming fancies
        That keep her from her rest.
MACBETH                               Cure her of that.          40
        Canst thou not minister to a mind diseased,
        Pluck from the memory a rooted sorrow,
        Raze out the written troubles of the brain,
        And with some sweet oblivious antidote
        Cleanse the stuffed bosom of that perilous stuff         45
        Which weighs upon the heart?
DOCTOR                               Therein the patient
        Must minister to himself.
MACBETH  Throw physic to the dogs, I'll none of it.
        Come, put mine armour on; give me my staff. –
        Seyton, send out. – Doctor, the thanes fly from me. –    50
        [*To Attendant*] Come sir, dispatch. – If thou couldst,
            doctor, cast
        The water of my land, find her disease,
        And purge it to a sound and pristine health,
        I would applaud thee to the very echo

*Macbeth leaves, calling for his armour. The Doctor determines to desert. Malcolm orders the army to use branches to camouflage their approach to Dunsinane. He reports many desertions from Macbeth's army.*

Gustave Doré's 1870 vision of Malcolm's army advancing, screened by branches from Birnam Wood. Work out how, in your own production, you could stage the approach of the camouflaged army.

**cynne** senna, a plant to purge (cleanse) the body
**bane** ruin
**chambers** bedrooms (Duncan was murdered in his bedroom)
**shadow** conceal
**discovery/Err in report of us** reconnaissance reports wrong about our numbers

**setting down before't** siege
**more and less . . . revolt** nobles and ordinary soldiers have deserted him
**constrainèd things** unwilling conscript soldiers

That should applaud again. – Pull't off, I say! –    55
What rhubarb, cynne, or what purgative drug
Would scour these English hence? Hear'st thou of them?
DOCTOR  Ay, my good lord; your royal preparation
Makes us hear something.
MACBETH                             Bring it after me. –
I will not be afraid of death and bane,    60
Till Birnam Forest come to Dunsinane.
                              [*Exeunt all but Doctor*]
DOCTOR  Were I from Dunsinane away and clear,
Profit again should hardly draw me here.        *Exit*


# ACT 5    SCENE 4
## Near Birnam Wood


Drum and colours. Enter MALCOLM, SIWARD, MACDUFF, Siward's
son, MENTEITH, CAITHNESS, ANGUS, and SOLDIERS, marching

MALCOLM  Cousins, I hope the days are near at hand
That chambers will be safe.
MENTEITH                             We doubt it nothing.
SIWARD  What wood is this before us?
MENTEITH                             The Wood of Birnam.
MALCOLM  Let every soldier hew him down a bough,
And bear't before him; thereby shall we shadow    5
The numbers of our host and make discovery
Err in report of us.
A SOLDIER              It shall be done.
SIWARD  We learn no other but the confident tyrant
Keeps still in Dunsinane and will endure
Our setting down before't.
MALCOLM                         'Tis his main hope,    10
For where there is advantage to be given,
Both more and less have given him the revolt,
And none serve with him but constrainèd things
Whose hearts are absent too.

*Siward advises against over-optimism. Macbeth defies the siege. Only desertions stop him openly facing Malcolm's army. He has almost lost any sense of fear. Seyton brings news of Lady Macbeth's death.*

## 1 'I have supped full with horrors' (in pairs)

The sound of women mourning prompts Macbeth to reflect that he has lost almost all sense of fear (lines 9–15). Once, an owl's shriek or a horror story would make his blood run cold and his hair stand on end. Now he can no longer be frightened.

Illustrate line 13 by making a collage of newspaper cuttings and other pictures.

## 2 'The queen, my lord, is dead' (in pairs)

How did Lady Macbeth die? At the end of the play, Malcolm reports that she committed suicide, but no one can be sure that is true (because history is written by the victors). Talk together about how you think she met her death, then choose one or more of the following:

a  write her dying speech
b  interview one of her waiting-women for her story
c  write an official communiqué or press release by the palace
d  devise a death scene involving up to four actors.

**just censures ... event** rightful
  claims decide the result
**owe** own, have won
**Thoughts speculative ...**
  **arbitrate** thinking won't
  determine the matter, but battle
  will

**ague** fever
**forced** reinforced
**my fell of hair** every hair on my
  body
**treatise** story
**Direness** horror
**start** frighten

MACDUFF                           Let our just censures
    Attend the true event and put we on                 15
    Industrious soldiership.
SIWARD                      The time approaches
    That will with due decision make us know
    What we shall say we have and what we owe;
    Thoughts speculative their unsure hopes relate,
    But certain issue strokes must arbitrate.           20
    Towards which, advance the war.

*Exeunt, marching*

## ACT 5    SCENE 5
## Dunsinane Castle

*Enter* MACBETH, SEYTON, *and soldiers, with drum and colours*

MACBETH  Hang out our banners on the outward walls;
    The cry is still, 'They come.' Our castle's strength
    Will laugh a siege to scorn; here let them lie
    Till famine and the ague eat them up.
    Were they not forced with those that should be ours,    5
    We might have met them dareful, beard to beard,
    And beat them backward home.
    *A cry within of women*
                          What is that noise?
SEYTON  It is the cry of women, my good lord.
MACBETH  I have almost forgot the taste of fears;
    The time has been, my senses would have cooled    10
    To hear a night-shriek and my fell of hair
    Would at a dismal treatise rouse and stir
    As life were in't. I have supped full with horrors;
    Direness familiar to my slaughterous thoughts
    Cannot once start me. Wherefore was that cry?    15
SEYTON  The queen, my lord, is dead.

*His wife's death sets Macbeth brooding on life's futility. A messenger tells that Birnam Wood is moving towards Dunsinane. Macbeth doubts the Apparition's ambiguous words. He determines to die fighting.*

### 1 'Tomorrow, and tomorrow, and tomorrow'
(in small groups)

Lines 18–27 are world-famous. It's worthwhile spending a good deal of time exploring them in different ways. Aim at the most dramatic presentation of Macbeth's soliloquy you can create. Here are just a few suggestions to help you:

a learn them by heart and present them as a radio broadcast

b share them out between the group and explore different ways of speaking them (sadly, angrily, fearfully, wonderingly . . . )

c mime or tableau each section

d pass them as secretly whispered messages among members of the group

e express them as world-weary, bleak fatalism

f decide to whom he speaks: the audience? Seyton, a picture? Or . . . ?

g try saying the sections in a different order from the one in which they are written. Talk about the difference it makes.

The most valuable method will be the one you invent for yourself.

### 2 What did the messenger see? (in pairs)

One person is the messenger at his guard post. He can see Birnam Wood. The other is the captain of the guard, who cannot see the wood. Improvise their conversation from a minute or two before the first movement of Malcolm's army.

---

**watch** period of guard duty
**anon** soon
**cling** wither
**sooth** true
**I pull in resolution** I lose confidence

**equivocation** double-talk
**avouches** says is true
**tarrying** waiting
**th'estate o'th'world** the universe
**harness** armour

MACBETH                                    She should have died hereafter;
            There would have been a time for such a word.
            Tomorrow, and tomorrow, and tomorrow
            Creeps in this petty pace from day to day
            To the last syllable of recorded time;                          20
            And all our yesterdays have lighted fools
            The way to dusty death. Out, out, brief candle,
            Life's but a walking shadow, a poor player
            That struts and frets his hour upon the stage
            And then is heard no more. It is a tale                          25
            Told by an idiot, full of sound and fury
            Signifying nothing.

                        *Enter a* MESSENGER

            Thou com'st to use thy tongue: thy story quickly.
MESSENGER Gracious my lord,
            I should report that which I say I saw,                         30
            But know not how to do't.
MACBETH                           Well, say, sir.
MESSENGER As I did stand my watch upon the hill
            I looked toward Birnam and anon methought
            The wood began to move.
MACBETH                            Liar and slave!
MESSENGER Let me endure your wrath if't be not so;                          35
            Within this three mile may you see it coming.
            I say, a moving grove.
MACBETH                         If thou speak'st false,
            Upon the next tree shall thou hang alive
            Till famine cling thee; if thy speech be sooth,
            I care not if thou dost for me as much.                         40
            I pull in resolution and begin
            To doubt th'equivocation of the fiend
            That lies like truth. 'Fear not, till Birnam Wood
            Do come to Dunsinane', and now a wood
            Comes toward Dunsinane. Arm, arm, and out!                      45
            If this which he avouches does appear,
            There is nor flying hence nor tarrying here.
            I 'gin to be aweary of the sun
            And wish th'estate o'th'world were now undone.
            Ring the alarum bell! Blow wind, come wrack;                    50
            At least we'll die with harness on our back.        *Exeunt*

*Malcolm instructs his troops to throw aside their camouflage of branches. He
issues orders for battle. Macbeth compares himself to a baited bear. He
is challenged by Young Siward.*

## 1 Battle plans

Malcolm orders the onslaught on Macbeth 'According to our order'
(the battle plan, Scene 6, lines 1–6). Draw up the battle plan: it is
usually a written order with a map.

Into battle. Roman Polanski's 1971 film showed the English army about to
attack Macbeth's castle at Dunsinane.

**leafy screens** tree branches
(camouflage)

**clamorous harbingers** noisy
forerunners (trumpet blasts)
***Alarums*** noise of battle

# ACT 5   SCENE 6
## Outside Dunsinane Castle

*Drum and colours. Enter* MALCOLM, SIWARD, MACDUFF, *and their*
*army, with boughs*

MALCOLM  Now near enough; your leafy screens throw down
    And show like those you are. You, worthy uncle,
    Shall with my cousin your right noble son
    Lead our first battle. Worthy Macduff and we
    Shall take upon's what else remains to do,         5
    According to our order.
SIWARD                    Fare you well.
    Do we but find the tyrant's power tonight,
    Let us be beaten if we cannot fight.
MACDUFF  Make all our trumpets speak; give them all breath,
    Those clamorous harbingers of blood and death.     10
                                *Exeunt*

*Alarums continued*

# ACT 5   SCENE 7
## Near the castle gate

*Enter* MACBETH

MACBETH  They have tied me to a stake; I cannot fly,
    But bear-like I must fight the course. What's he
    That was not born of woman? Such a one
    Am I to fear, or none.

*Enter* YOUNG SIWARD

YOUNG SIWARD  What is thy name?                 5
MACBETH  Thou'lt be afraid to hear it.
YOUNG SIWARD  No, though thou call'st thyself a hotter name
    Than any is in hell.

*Macbeth kills Young Siward and boasts that no man born of woman can kill him. Macduff refuses to fight with mercenaries and seeks only Macbeth. Siward invites Malcolm to enter Macbeth's surrendered castle.*

## 1 Macbeth the warrior (in small groups)

Many professional productions call on the services of a fight arranger, who works out how a stage fight can be both dramatic and safe. Work out the moves for lines 5–14. Remember: safety is vital! Rehearse in slow motion.

## 2 Action and words (in groups of four to six)

Macduff speaks lines 15–24 on an apparently empty stage, but most directors seek to create the impression that a battle is raging. They have to ensure that the lines can be heard and can be related to the action.

Take the lines a short section at a time, and work out what actions (or sounds) would fit best. You may wish to have other actors come on stage at certain points, to give Macduff's sentences extra, visible meaning. Show your acted version to the class.

## 3 'The tyrant's people on both sides do fight' (in pairs)

One of the tragedies of civil war is that members of the same family can find themselves on opposite sides (line 26). Create a Scots family that finds its loyalties split by Macbeth's rule. Father is pitted against son, brother against brother. Invent a scene where father meets son on the battlefield. What happens?

---

**abhorrèd** detested
**kerns** lightly armed soldiers
**whose arms . . . staves**
  mercenaries (who fight only for pay)
**staves** wooden weapons

**undeeded** unused (having performed no deeds)
**bruited** announced
**gently rendered** surrendered with little fighting
**strike beside us** deliberately miss us

MACBETH                          My name's Macbeth.

YOUNG SIWARD  The devil himself could not pronounce a title
    More hateful to mine ear.

MACBETH                                No, nor more fearful.                    10

YOUNG SIWARD  Thou liest, abhorrèd tyrant; with my sword
    I'll prove the lie thou speak'st.

          *Fight, and young Siward slain*

MACBETH                              Thou wast born of woman.
    But swords I smile at, weapons laugh to scorn,
    Brandished by man that's of a woman born.

            *Exit [with young Siward's body]*

       *Alarums. Enter* MACDUFF

MACDUFF  That way the noise is. Tyrant, show thy face!           15
    If thou be'st slain, and with no stroke of mine,
    My wife and children's ghosts will haunt me still.
    I cannot strike at wretched kerns whose arms
    Are hired to bear their staves; either thou, Macbeth,
    Or else my sword with an unbattered edge                    20
    I sheath again undeeded. There thou shouldst be;
    By this great clatter, one of greatest note
    Seems bruited. Let me find him, Fortune,
    And more I beg not.                                    *Exit*

      *Alarums. Enter* MALCOLM *and* SIWARD

SIWARD  This way, my lord; the castle's gently rendered.          25
    The tyrant's people on both sides do fight;
    The noble thanes do bravely in the war.
    The day almost itself professes yours,
    And little is to do.

MALCOLM                        We have met with foes
    That strike beside us.

SIWARD                            Enter, sir, the castle.           30

               *Exeunt*

       *Alarum*

*Facing Macduff, Macbeth boasts that no naturally born man can kill him, but Macduff reveals his own Caesarean birth. Dismayed, Macbeth refuses to fight. Macduff threatens that he will be exhibited in captivity.*

'Turn, hell-hound, turn.' Macbeth finally comes face to face with his nemesis (Royal Shakespeare Company, 1982).

## 1 Macbeth's luck runs out

Macbeth faces final disaster. His luck ('charmèd life') has run out. The play itself has gained a notorious reputation for being unlucky. Many actors refuse to speak its name, calling it instead 'the Scottish play', because they think to name *Macbeth* will bring bad luck. There are many stories of accidents associated with productions of the play. The worst was in May 1849 at a performance of *Macbeth* in New York. It provoked a bloody riot which resulted in twenty-two deaths and over 150 injuries.

**play the Roman fool** commit suicide (defeated Roman generals fell on their swords)
**terms** words
**intrenchant** uncuttable
**impress** mark, strike

**crests** helmets, heads
**angel** devil, Satan
**Untimely ripped** prematurely delivered (by Caesarean section)
**palter with us in a double sense** equivocate with double meanings

# ACT 5   SCENE 8
## Outside Dunsinane Castle

Enter MACBETH

MACBETH  Why should I play the Roman fool and die
    On mine own sword? Whiles I see lives, the gashes
    Do better upon them.

*Enter* MACDUFF

MACDUFF                 Turn, hell-hound, turn.
MACBETH  Of all men else I have avoided thee,
    But get thee back, my soul is too much charged      5
    With blood of thine already.
MACDUFF               I have no words;
    My voice is in my sword, thou bloodier villain
    Than terms can give thee out.
                      *Fight. Alarum*
MACBETH               Thou losest labour.
    As easy mayst thou the intrenchant air
    With thy keen sword impress as make me bleed.      10
    Let fall thy blade on vulnerable crests;
    I bear a charmèd life which must not yield
    To one of woman born.
MACDUFF             Despair thy charm,
    And let the angel whom thou still hast served
    Tell thee, Macduff was from his mother's womb      15
    Untimely ripped.
MACBETH  Accursèd be that tongue that tells me so,
    For it hath cowed my better part of man;
    And be these juggling fiends no more believed
    That palter with us in a double sense,      20
    That keep the word of promise to our ear
    And break it to our hope. I'll not fight with thee.
MACDUFF  Then yield thee coward,
    And live to be the show and gaze o'th'time.
    We'll have thee, as our rarer monsters are,      25
    Painted upon a pole and underwrit,
    'Here may you see the tyrant.'

*Macbeth determines to go down fighting, and is killed. Siward reports light casualties. On being told that his son is dead, Siward's concern is to know if Young Siward died bravely.*

### 1 Shakespeare's film script? (in groups of six to twelve)

Scenes 4–8 are like a film script: a series of brief action-filled episodes. They show different aspects of the fighting, and build up a vivid impression of the fast-moving battle. Identify the different sequences in the five scenes, and work out a film script. Remember: battle scenes should give the impression of violent action, but they should be perfectly safe for the actors. Locate places in your school or college where you could film.

### 2 Death rather than captivity (in small groups)

Macbeth realises that the end has come. The Apparitions have falsely raised his hopes by their double-talk. They have both lied and spoken the truth about Birnam Wood and 'no man of woman born'. Macbeth chooses to die fighting because he cannot bear the thought of being subservient to Malcolm and exhibited like a fairground show.

How does Macbeth's choice affect your view of him? Does choosing death give him a kind of nobility and dignity? Talk together about under what conditions you think death is preferable to captivity.

### 3 Report the battle

Choose one of the following ways of reporting the final battle:

a by the wounded Captain from Act 1 Scene 2
b by the Witches
c in a report for one of Scotland's national newspapers
d as a war diary kept by an ordinary soldier.

---

**baited** mocked, tormented like a chained bear
**Retreat, and flourish** trumpet call at the end of battle, fanfare
**go off** die

**prowess** bravery
**unshrinking station** place of no retreat
**Had he his hurts before?** were his wounds on the front of his body?

MACBETH                              I will not yield
　　　To kiss the ground before young Malcolm's feet
　　　And to be baited with the rabble's curse.
　　　Though Birnam Wood be come to Dunsinane                30
　　　And thou opposed being of no woman born,
　　　Yet I will try the last. Before my body,
　　　I throw my warlike shield. Lay on, Macduff,
　　　And damned be him that first cries, 'Hold, enough!'
　　　　　　　　　　　　*Exeunt[,] fighting. Alarums*

*Enter [Macbeth and Macduff,] fighting[,] and Macbeth slain*

　　　　　　　　　*[Exit Macduff, with Macbeth's body]*


# ACT 5    SCENE 9
## Dunsinane Castle

*Retreat, and flourish. Enter with drum and colours,* MALCOLM,
*SIWARD, ROSS, thanes, and soldiers*

MALCOLM I would the friends we miss were safe arrived.
SIWARD Some must go off. And yet by these I see,
　　　So great a day as this is cheaply bought.
MALCOLM Macduff is missing and your noble son.
ROSS Your son, my lord, has paid a soldier's debt;                5
　　　He only lived but till he was a man,
　　　The which no sooner had his prowess confirmed
　　　In the unshrinking station where he fought,
　　　But like a man he died.
SIWARD                          Then he is dead?
ROSS Ay, and brought off the field. Your cause of sorrow        10
　　　Must not be measured by his worth, for then
　　　It hath no end.
SIWARD                          Had he his hurts before?
ROSS Ay, on the front.

*Macduff displays Macbeth's severed head, and hails Malcolm as King of Scotland. Malcolm rewards his nobles for their services, creating them earls. He invites everyone to his coronation at Scone.*

### 1 Siward the father (in groups of three)

Take parts and read lines 1–20. Talk together about Siward's reaction to his son's death, and what this episode adds to the play. Do you think you would feel the same in Siward's place?

### 2 Macbeth's head

Often, audiences are not sure whether to be appalled or to laugh at the sight of Macbeth's severed head. Imagine that you are designer of a production. Decide what you will do about Macbeth's head.

### 3 'Cruel ministers' (in groups of six to ten)

Macbeth's agents are to be hunted down and tried (line 35). Round up Seyton, the 'cream-faced loon' and the murderers of Banquo and Macduff's family. Hold a fair trial. What sentences are passed?

### 4 The Witches meet Malcolm (in groups of four to six)

Invent a further scene where Malcolm, on his way to Scone, meets the Witches. What happens?

### 5 Scotland under Malcolm (in groups of six to twelve)

Some critics argue that Malcolm's victory restores peace, order, justice and harmony to Scotland. Others claim that Scotland will still be torn apart by the power struggles of rival warlords. Prepare two versions of the final minute of the play the audience will see. One version shows the prospect of a peaceful future; the second shows a future of war and oppression. You might wish to prepare a third version showing that the witches are about to intervene again.

---

**knell is knolled** death bell is rung
**paid his score** settled his account
(died as a man)
**usurper** illegal king
**compassed with thy kingdom's
pearl** surrounded by the nobility
of Scotland

**reckon with your several loves**
calculate what I owe each of you
**be planted newly . . . time** begin
the new era

SIWARD   Why then, God's soldier be he;
    Had I as many sons as I have hairs,     15
    I would not wish them to a fairer death.
    And so his knell is knolled.
MALCOLM         He's worth more sorrow,
    And that I'll spend for him.
SIWARD          He's worth no more;
    They say he parted well and paid his score,
    And so God be with him. Here comes newer comfort.  20

   *Enter* MACDUFF, *with Macbeth's head*

MACDUFF   Hail, king, for so thou art. Behold where stands
    Th'usurper's cursèd head. The time is free.
    I see thee compassed with thy kingdom's pearl,
    That speak my salutation in their minds;
    Whose voices I desire aloud with mine.     25
    Hail, King of Scotland.
ALL         Hail, King of Scotland.
      *Flourish*
MALCOLM   We shall not spend a large expense of time
    Before we reckon with your several loves
    And make us even with you. My thanes and kinsmen,
    Henceforth be earls, the first that ever Scotland  30
    In such an honour named. What's more to do
    Which would be planted newly with the time, –
    As calling home our exiled friends abroad
    That fled the snares of watchful tyranny,
    Producing forth the cruel ministers     35
    Of this dead butcher and his fiend-like queen,
    Who, as 'tis thought, by self and violent hands
    Took off her life, – this and what needful else
    That calls upon us, by the grace of Grace
    We will perform in measure, time, and place.   40
    So, thanks to all at once and to each one,
    Whom we invite to see us crowned at Scone.
      *Flourish*

           *Exeunt*

# Looking back at the play
*Activities for groups or individuals*

## 1 A play of darkness

Darkness intensifies the dramatic effect of the action and language. Look back over each of the twenty-seven scenes, and identify which ones you think take place at night or in darkness.

## 2 Where the place?

Every director and editor of the play has to decide where each scene is set (Shakespeare himself did not write the locations suggested in this script). Turn to each scene heading and decide whether or not you think it is appropriate.

## 3 Citations for bravery and campaign medals

After every battle, medals are awarded. Design a set of medals for Malcolm's campaign against Macbeth. Write the citations for several soldiers who are to be awarded medals (a citation is an account of the brave actions performed by an individual in battle).

## 4 Point of view

Modern directors are often accused of 'concept theatre', in which one dominant idea or concept affects every aspect of their production. Usually the 'accusers' have their own firm (but different) concept of how Shakespeare should be performed!

Imagine that you are a director. You wish to put on *Macbeth* from one of the following points of view:

Marxist (money underlies every human/social relationship)
Psychoanalytic (childhood experience underlies all adult behaviour)
Feminist (from a woman's perspective)
New Historicist (plays reveal the historical period of their writing)
Poetic-aesthetic (the beauty of the language is what matters)
Liberal humanist (freedom and human progress are the goals)
Brechtian (remind the audience they are watching a political play)

Work out how 'your' concept would present one or two scenes or episodes. Act them out.

## 5 'Foul whisperings are abroad'

Under any tyranny there are always seeds of resistance, however weak. Graffiti appears on walls, rumours circulate, underground pamphlets (samizdat) are published. Make up the 'resistance literature' that spreads throughout Macbeth's Scotland. Invent slogans, write resistance pamphlets, spread rumours.

## 6 Three viewpoints: choose one

a Write the Scottish Doctor's case notes on Lady Macbeth.
b Write a letter from Lady Macbeth's Gentlewoman to her brother or sister, telling about her mistress.
c What happened to the cream-faced loon? Make up the story of what he saw, his meeting with Macbeth, and what he did afterwards.

## 7 Every picture tells a story

Look back over the pictures in this script. Talk about why you think they have been chosen, and what each one suggests about the particular production it illustrates.

## 8 Where's Donaldbain?

Donaldbain has not returned with Malcolm's victorious army. Write his diary entry as he thinks about the news he has heard from Scotland. Show why he has not joined the victors.

## 9 A political cartoon

Some cartoonists are very clever at showing how matters of national politics and power can be expressed through drawings that only show individuals. Draw a cartoon that shows Macbeth, but also comments on the state of Scotland.

## 10 Cast the play

Most modern productions have fairly small casts. This means that some parts are 'doubled' (one actor plays several parts). Imagine that you are going to put on the play, but have only ten actors. Copy out the cast list and work out which parts you will double.

## 11 An unusual conversation!

Imagine that the historical Macbeth and William Shakespeare come back to life. They meet. Improvise their conversation.

# The meanings of *Macbeth*

There is no single 'right' way of thinking about or performing *Macbeth*. It has been hugely popular for almost four hundred years, performed many thousands of times in very different versions. Millions of words have been written about it since Shakespeare's time. It is impossible to reach a final answer to the question 'What is *Macbeth* about?' Because the play works on so many different levels, a multitude of interpretations are possible – all with a claim to truth.

The aim of this edition of *Macbeth* is to enable you to make up your own mind about the play. The following pages give possible starting points for thought and activity. All are invitations to explore further on your own or in a group, and so help you bring the play alive in your own imagination. The play is like a kaleidoscope. Every time it is performed or read, it reveals different shapes, patterns, meanings, interpretations. For example, *Macbeth* is:

**a** A historical thriller: a fast-moving action-packed murder story showing that crime does not pay.

**b** A psychological study of a murderer's mind: Macbeth constantly reveals his inmost thoughts.

**c** A play of political and social realism: showing how an oppressive hierarchical society systematically produces corrupt individuals.

**d** A play of illusions: showing the effect on human beings of the mysterious or supernatural (the Witches, the dagger, and so on).

**e** A play of ideas or themes: for example, 'appearance and reality'.

**f** A dramatic poem: showing how a poet of genius uses language and imagery to great imaginative effect.

**g** A tragedy: the portrayal of the fall of a great man because of a fatal flaw in his character (Macbeth's ambition causes his death).

Choose one of the above interpretations:
*Either*: tell the story of Macbeth from that point of view
    *Or*: work out a performance of the play seen from that viewpoint.

# The action of *Macbeth*

Here are three examples of how students have performed or written about the action of the play.

## A *Macbeth* in five acts

Act 1    The Witches' predictions
Act 2    The murder of Duncan
Act 3    The murder of Banquo
Act 4    The murder of Lady Macduff
Act 5    Retribution: crime doesn't pay

## B A student's poem

(Acted out in the seven letters of Macbeth's name: seven lines, seven events.)

Meeting three Witches on the blasted heath
Ambition grew and poisoned brave Macbeth.
Cunning, his wife led him to stab the king,
Banquo was next. His Ghost spoiled everything.
Evil now reigned as Macbeth killed all dead,
Tyranny ended when Macduff saw red.
Hope came with Malcolm, Macbeth lost his head.

## C The play in twelve actions

1   Battle: Macbeth's bravery
2   Three predictions
3   The Macbeths plot together
4   Murder: Duncan
5   Murder: Banquo
6   The banquet: Banquo's Ghost
7   The cauldron: the Apparitions make predictions
8   Murder: Lady Macduff
9   England: planning Macbeth's overthrow
10  Sleepwalking: a nightmare recap
11  Birnam Wood: siege and battle
12  Macbeth's death: Malcolm's triumph

Write or act out your own *Macbeth* as a short story, play or poem. Use the three examples above as guides, or invent your own version.

# The themes of *Macbeth*

Themes are ideas or concepts of fundamental importance that recur throughout the play, linking together plot, characters and language. Themes echo, reinforce, and comment upon each other and the whole play. Some major themes in *Macbeth* are:

**Ambition:** ruthless seeking after power by Macbeth, urged on by his wife. It is the tragic flaw that causes his downfall ('I have no spur/To prick the sides of my intent, but only/Vaulting ambition').

**Evil:** the urge to destroy whatever is good; the brooding presence of murderous intention and action ('Fair is foul, and foul is fair').

**Order and disorder:** the struggle to maintain or destroy social and natural bonds; the destruction of morality and mutual trust ('Uproar the universal peace, confound/All unity on earth').

**Appearance and reality:** evil lurks behind fair looks. Deceit and hypocrisy mean that appearances cannot be trusted (Lady Macbeth's 'Look like th' innocent flower,/But be the serpent under 't').

**Equivocation:** telling deliberately misleading half-truths ('th' equivocation of the fiend/That lies like truth').

**Violence and tyranny:** warfare, destruction and oppression recur throughout the play ('pour the sweet milk of concord into hell').

**Guilt and conscience:** Macbeth knows that what he does is wrong. He does it none the less, and suffers agonies of conscience as a result ('O, full of scorpions is my mind').

**Man:** the violent cut-throat feudal society of hierarchical male power breeds bloody stereotypes of what it is to be a man. 'I dare do all that may become a man', says Macbeth, contemplating murder. However, the play offers other visions of manhood: 'But I must also feel it as a man', cries Macduff, weeping at news of his family's murder.

Other themes are: the supernatural (see pages 166–7); retribution (Macbeth has to pay for his crimes); innocence and goodness; harmony and grace (interpreting the play as a parable on the loss of God's grace); fate and free will; loyalty and patriotism; over-confidence ('security').

# Imagery in *Macbeth*

*Macbeth* is rich in imagery: vivid words and phrases that conjure up emotionally charged mental pictures. They carry powerful significance, far deeper than their surface meanings.

**Darkness and light**: 'Dark night strangles the travelling lamp'; 'Come, thick night . . .'.

**Blood**: the word 'blood' occurs frequently throughout the play.

**Babies and children**: signifying vulnerability and innocence.

**Disease and medicine**: Scotland is sick under Macbeth's rule, and individuals are corrupted ('brain-sickly'). But individuals and societies may be cured ('med'cine of the sickly weal').

**Feasting and hospitality**: eating together is a sign of friendship and community. Macbeth's disrupted banquet signifies the moral dissolution of both himself and Scotland.

**Sleep**: the Macbeths lack the healing balm of sleep ('these terrible dreams/That shake us nightly'; Lady Macbeth's sleepwalking).

**Animals, birds and insects**: the many references to ominous creatures heighten the destructive, fearful atmosphere (for example, the cauldron scene).

**Clothes**: Macbeth's usurpation of the throne of Scotland dresses him in 'borrowed robes' (illustrating the theme of deceptive appearances).

Other images include: acting and theatre ('a poor player'); eyes ('the eye of childhood'); hunting and 'sport' ('bear-like I must fight the course'); hands ('will these hands ne'er be clean?').

Choose one theme or image. Make a list of language and actions in the play that illustrate it. Express your findings dramatically or visually, for example, a short play or mime, or a wall display (for example, 'order and disorder' might include: the blasted heath; the murder of Duncan; Lady Macbeth's 'fill me . . . topfull/Of direst cruelty'; the cauldron ingredients; Duncan's horses eating each other . . . and so on).

# History into drama

*History's Macbeth*: eleventh-century Scotland was a violent and troubled country. Feuding families and clans fought to control trade and territory. The castle was the power base of each rival war-lord (thane). Political murder and revenge killings were commonplace. Marauding Vikings and Norsemen raided constantly.

Macbeth was born into this violent world in 1005, son of the great family that ruled Moray and Ross. His own father was murdered by his cousins. Macbeth married Gruach, granddaughter to a High King of Scotland. They had no children of their own. There is no historical evidence about Lady Macbeth's influence on her husband.

Duncan's rule had been ineffectual and unpopular. He was thirty-eight when he was killed, possibly by Macbeth, who was elected High King of Scotland in 1040. Macbeth ruled for seventeen years – for the first ten as a competent, reforming king. He gave Scotland a long period of comparative peace and stability. There is no evidence that Macbeth dabbled in witchcraft; indeed, he was a strong supporter of the Church.

Duncan's son Malcolm invaded Scotland in 1054, supported by the English King, Edward the Confessor. Macbeth was killed on 15 August 1057 at Peel Ring, Lumphanan in Mar. He was buried at Iona, the sacred burial place of the Kings of Scotland.

*Holinshed's Macbeth*: Shakespeare was a playwright, not a historian. But he knew that history provided splendid material for plays: war, conflict, ambition, the downfall of great rulers. Earlier in his career he had written his English history plays drawing on the stories in Raphael Holinshed's *Chronicles of England, Scotland and Ireland* (1587). Holinshed made uncritical use of earlier historians and believed that Tudor monarchy was the best form of government. His story of Macbeth now fired Shakespeare's imagination.

But Shakespeare never slavishly followed any source. He selected, altered and added to achieve maximum dramatic effect. He invented Lady Macbeth's sleepwalking and death, the banquet scene and Banquo's Ghost, and most of the cauldron scene. Shakespeare changed Duncan from an ineffectual king into an old and revered ruler, and omitted Macbeth's ten years of good rule.

# A *Macbeth* for King James?

King James I succeeded Queen Elizabeth I on the English throne in 1603. He was a member of the Stuart dynasty and already King of Scotland. *Macbeth* may have been performed before King James in 1606. It contains many echoes of James's interests:

*Banquo*: Holinshed included an elaborate family tree of the Stuart dynasty, showing King James's descent from Banquo. Shakespeare has a single stage direction: 'A show of eight kings, and the last with a glass in his hand; Banquo's Ghost following' (James was the ninth Stuart monarch). Unlike Holinshed, Shakespeare did not make Banquo an accomplice to Duncan's murder. Instead, he lays full responsibility on the Macbeths. This alteration presumably pleased King James, who hated regicides (king-killers). In fact, Banquo never existed. He was invented as the source of Stuart royalty.

*Witchcraft*: King James's interest in witchcraft was well known (see page 167). He visited Oxford in 1605 and was greeted by three witches who hailed him as the descendant of Banquo.

*The Gunpowder Plot, 5 November 1605*: a medal was struck to commemorate the king's escape. It showed a snake concealed by flowers. The Plot is believed to be referred to in Act 2 Scene 3, line 50 ('dire combustion'). Everard Digby, one of the conspirators, was a favourite of the king (mirroring Cawdor?).

*Equivocation*: a Catholic priest, Henry Garnet, was accused in 1606 of treason for involvement in the Gunpowder Plot. He was found to have committed perjury (given false evidence), but claimed to have the right to equivocate (tell deliberately misleading half-truths) in self-defence. Equivocation is a major theme of the play (see page 162).

*Honours*: Malcolm's gift of earldoms at the end of the play reflects King James's liberal giving of English titles to his Scottish supporters.

Divide the class into three groups. Each group takes one of the following positions on *Macbeth* and argues their case:

a Shakespeare is flattering King James in *Macbeth*.
b Shakespeare is critically appraising kingship in *Macbeth*.
c *Macbeth* reflects matters of public interest in 1605–6.

# Witches and witchcraft

Throughout Shakespeare's life, witches and witchcraft were the object of morbid and fevered fascination. A veritable witch-mania characterised the reign of Elizabeth I. Persecution reached terrifying proportions. Between 1560 and 1603 hundreds of people (nearly all women) were convicted as witches and executed.

Although some voices were raised against this superstitious and barbarous persecution, most people believed in witches. Hundreds of pamphlets describing the lurid details of witchcraft trials were printed. They enjoyed enormous sales: the equivalent of today's popular newspapers, or films about exorcism and the supernatural.

Witches were credited with diabolical powers. They could predict the future, fly, sail in sieves, bring on night in daytime, cause fogs and tempests, and kill animals. They cursed enemies with fatal wasting diseases, induced nightmares and sterility, and could take demonic possession of any individual they chose. Witches could raise evil spirits by concocting a horrible brew with nauseating ingredients.

It was believed that witches allowed the Devil to suck their blood in exchange for a 'familiar': a bird, reptile or beast as an evil servant. Accused witches were examined for the 'Devil's mark', a red mark on their body from which Satan had sucked blood ('damned spot').

In 1604 an Act of Parliament decreed that anyone found guilty of practising witchcraft should be executed. Single old women who kept cats were in constant danger of being accused of witchcraft. If they were convicted, they endured torture and death by hanging or burning at the stake.

This cruel persecution was fuelled by an ugly mixture of superstition, misogyny (hatred of women) and a firm conviction that religion and morality were being upheld. Those who confessed to being witches did so under torture or because they were in the grip of delusions that are recognised today as psychiatric disorders.

- Identify in the script the beliefs about witches listed above.
- Discuss whether *Macbeth* presents a crude stereotype of witches.
- Only once in the script does someone call the three weird sisters 'witches' (Act 1 Scene 3, line 5). Work out ways of performing them as other than the conventional stereotype of witches (see, for example, picture c on page 131).

King James was as fascinated by witchcraft as any of his subjects. In 1590 it was alleged that a group of witches tried to kill him. Their plot was discovered and they were brought to trial at North Berwick. The claims of one witch, Agnes Sampson, were sensational. She had collected toad venom to poison the king, christened a cat, tied parts of a dead man's body to it, sailed out to sea in a sieve and thrown cat and body-bits overboard to raise a storm to sink the king's ship.

King James personally interrogated one of the accused witches, Dr Fian. The poor doctor was horribly tortured: 'His nails upon all his fingers were riven and pulled off . . . his legs were crushed and beaten together as small as might be, and the bones and flesh so bruised that the blood and marrow spouted forth in great abundance.'

Fired by his experience at North Berwick, King James personally investigated other witchcraft cases. In 1597 he published *Demonology*, a book on witchcraft. When he became King of England in 1603 he ordered its immediate printing in London.

King James's England was a Christian country. Although deep divisions existed between Protestants and Catholics, nearly everyone believed literally in Heaven and Hell, and lived in fear of eternal damnation: a consequence of witchcraft. Many of those watching *Macbeth* saw in it the signs of a man and woman seized by demonic possession:

*Trance*: 'Look how our partner's rapt' (page 17, line 141).

*Changed appearance*: 'Why do you make such faces?' (page 85, line 67).

*Inability to pray*: '"Amen"/Stuck in my throat' (page 45, lines 35–6).

*Visions*: 'Is this a dagger which I see before me?' (page 41, line 33).

*Disturbed behaviour*: 'I have a strange infirmity' (page 85, line 86).

*Lack of fear*: 'I have almost forgot the taste of fears' (page 145, line 9).

*Indifference to life*: 'She should have died hereafter' (page 147, line 16).

*Invitations to evil spirits to possess one's body*: 'Come, you spirits' (page 25, line 38).

Shakespeare's audience would also hear in *Macbeth* many echoes of their Christian faith. The religious imagery would remind them of the damnation that awaited those who challenged Christian beliefs (for example, 'sacrilegious murder hath broke ope/The Lord's anointed temple').

# The language of *Macbeth*

## 1 Key words

Certain words recur throughout *Macbeth*, creating meaning, atmosphere and significance: for example, 'blood', 'fear', 'sleep', 'time',
'night', 'done', 'man'.

Choose one key word. Trace it through the play, listing each use in
its context. Work out a powerful way of reporting your findings.

## 2 Soliloquies

A soliloquy is a monologue spoken by a character who is alone (or
assumes that he or she is alone) on stage. It reveals their inner
thoughts and motives. Macbeth often 'thinks aloud': about half his
lines seem to be spoken to himself. But a soliloquy can be spoken
direct to the audience if the actor thinks it suitable.

- Identify the occasions where Macbeth seems to 'think aloud'.
  Decide whether you feel that he is speaking truthfully on each
  occasion.
- Experiment with different styles of speaking one of Macbeth's
  soliloquies: to the audience? to himself? to a stage prop?
- Invent a soliloquy for a minor character (for example, Seyton,
  Donaldbain).

## 3 Creating new words

Shakespeare had a great gift for making up new words. One estimate of
his vocabulary is 30,000 words (most of us get by with about 6,000).
One way in which he created words is very simple: by the use of the
hyphen. *Macbeth* is full of hyphenated words, many so familiar that we
do not recognise them as Shakespeare's (new-born, firm-set, new-
hatched, live-long, bare-faced, cut-throat, earth-bound, lily-livered,
bear-like).

Search through the play for hyphenated words. List all you find.
Then write a story (for example, a re-telling of *Macbeth* or a story of
your own) using some of those hyphenated words. Add your own new
words, created using the hyphen.

## 4 Verse

The play is written mainly in blank verse (unrhyming lines with a five-beat rhythm: 'iambic pentameter'). Each line has five iambs (feet), each with a stressed (/) and unstressed (×) syllable:

'So fair / and foul/a day/I have/not seen'

Shakespeare uses blank verse very flexibly, making the rhythm of each speech appropriate to the meaning, the mood, and the speaker.

The Witches almost always speak in four-beat rhythm. This incantatory style is particularly appropriate to spells and the supernatural:

'Fair is foul, and foul is fair'

Choose a favourite speech. By reading it in different ways, discover how the rhythm of the verse is appropriate to the speaker's meaning and mood (for example, fearful apprehension, devious plotting, anguished confusion, sarcastic questioning, reflective self-questioning). Write four to eight lines of your own in the same style.

## 5 Prose

Shakespeare usually put prose into the mouths of his 'low-status' characters, but he was never afraid to break that rule. There are five prose sequences in the play: Macbeth's letter to his wife; the Porter; Macbeth's conversation with the Murderers; part of Lady Macduff's conversation with her son; Lady Macbeth's sleepwalking. Consider each prose passage in turn. Talk together about:

a  how each prose example differs from the other
b  the suitability of prose (why is it used rather than verse?)
c  the dramatic effect of switching from verse to prose at those points.

## 6 Antithesis

The Witches chant: 'When the battle's lost and won . . . Fair is foul and foul is fair'. Each close juxtaposing of opposites (lost/won, fair/foul) is an antithesis. You will find antitheses everywhere in the play, but the Porter scene and Macbeth's 'If it were done . . .' (Act 1 Scene 7, lines 1–28) are particularly rich.

Choose a scene or speech and identify the antitheses. As you speak the language, find physical ways to show the contrasts (for example, by 'weighing' them with your hands, or pushing and pulling arms with a partner).

# Staging *Macbeth*

The story goes that *Macbeth* was first performed before King James I at Hampton Court in 1606. No one knows for certain if that is true. The first record of a production was written by Simon Forman, who described a performance he saw at the Globe Theatre on Bankside in 1611, when he claims to have seen Macbeth and Banquo on horseback. Perhaps he was reminded of a picture in Holinshed's *Chronicles* (see page 164) by the sound of horses' hooves. The actors probably added other sound effects: the whining, croaking and mewing of the Witches' familiars; thunder; the owl's screech and the clanging of the dreadful bell.

Since Shakespeare's time, *Macbeth* has been an ever-popular play. The diarist Samuel Pepys saw it at least three times in the 1660s and thought it excellent. But like all of Shakespeare's plays, *Macbeth* has been re-written, revised and adapted through the centuries to meet the tastes and the social and political circumstances of different times.

Sir William Davenant (who claimed to be Shakespeare's illegitimate son) presented a radically changed version from that in the First Folio of 1623 (see page 172). A record of his 1672 production reads:

> The Tragedy of Macbeth, altered by Sir William Davenant; being dressed in all its finery, as new clothes, new scenes, machines, as flyings for the witches; with all the singing and dancing . . . being all excellently performed being in the nature of an opera.

*Macbeth* became a musical spectacular with the Witches as a series of comic turns as they flew, danced and sang in ever-increasing numbers. One nineteenth-century production put over a hundred witches on stage! There was little hesitation about cutting, amending or adding to the 1623 Folio version. Davenant cut the Porter and the Doctors, had Seyton change sides at the end, and altered the language so as not to offend his audience of gentry. Scenes were added: Lady Macbeth and Lady Macduff talked together. Macduff's role was greatly enlarged at the expense of Malcolm's. The Witches turned up to support Macduff against Macbeth.

Although there were attempts to return to the 1623 Folio script, the operatic additions to *Macbeth* persisted. Even those who wished to return to Shakespeare's version could not resist the temptation to alter. The great eighteenth-century actor David Garrick wrote a long dying speech for Macbeth, expressing sorrow and self-condemnation. Nineteenth-century productions tried to depict medieval Scotland in what they thought were authentic sets and costumes. The on-stage castles in *Macbeth* matched the Gothic mansions that the newly rich industrialists were building in the Scottish Highlands.

Only in the twentieth century were the spectacular operatic effects removed. Most modern productions are based on the 1623 Folio script, but in every production some adaptation takes place. The play has been set in nineteenth-century Cuba, Hitler's Germany, and in the Great War of 1914–18. It has been adapted as classical opera (by Verdi) and rock opera (see page 37).

Although spectacular productions are now rare, they can be immensely successful. An all-black 1972 adaptation, *Umabatha*, designed for the open air, made *Macbeth* a play about Zulu identity in early nineteenth-century South Africa. Chanting, drumming, and rhythmically beating shields, a huge cast created a tribal *Macbeth* of immense ritual power. The Zulu warriors grieved, rejoiced, welcomed and fought throughout their own unique re-staging of Shakespeare's tragedy.

In 1976 the Royal Shakespeare Company played *Macbeth* in the round, without an interval. The production showed how a small cast, working in a small space with minimal props, can create an outstandingly imaginative *Macbeth*.

## Stage your own production of *Macbeth*

Talk together about the period and place in which you will set your play: medieval Scotland? a modern office? a fascist state? a 'timeless' setting? Then choose one or more of the following activities. Your finished assignment can be a file of drawings, notes and suggestions, or an active presentation.

- Design the set – how can it be used for particular scenes?
- Design the costumes – look at past examples, but invent your own.
- Design the publicity poster – make people want to see your play!
- Design the programme – layout? content? number of pages?
- Write character notes for actors' guidance.
- Work out a five-minute presentation to show potential sponsors.
- The local army commander agrees to lend you one hundred soldiers for your show – how will you use them?

# William Shakespeare 1564–1616

1564  Born Stratford-upon-Avon, eldest son of John and Mary Shakespeare.
1582  Married to Anne Hathaway of Shottery, near Stratford.
1583  Daughter, Susanna, born.
1585  Twins, son and daughter, Hamnet and Judith, born.
1592  First mention of Shakespeare in London. Robert Greene, another playwright, described Shakespeare as 'an upstart crow beautified with our feathers . . .'. Greene seems to have been jealous of Shakespeare. He mocked Shakespeare's name, calling him 'the only Shake-scene in a country' (presumably because Shakespeare was writing successful plays).
1595  A shareholder in 'The Lord Chamberlain's Men', an acting company that became extremely popular.
1596  Son Hamnet died, aged eleven.
       Father, John, granted arms (acknowledged as a gentleman).
1597  Bought New Place, the grandest house in Stratford.
1598  Acted in Ben Jonson's *Every Man in His Humour*.
1599  Globe Theatre opens on Bankside. Performances in the open air.
1601  Father, John, dies.
1603  James I granted Shakespeare's company a royal patent: 'The Lord Chamberlain's Men' became 'The King's Men' and played about twelve performances each year at court.
1607  Daughter, Susanna, marries Dr John Hall.
1608  Mother, Mary, dies.
1609  'The King's Men' begin performing indoors at Blackfriars Theatre.
1610  Probably returned from London to live in Stratford.
1616  Daughter, Judith, marries Thomas Quiney.
       Died. Buried in Holy Trinity Church, Stratford-upon-Avon.

## The plays and poems
(no one knows exactly when he wrote each play)

1589–1595  *The Two Gentlemen of Verona, The Taming of the Shrew, First, Second and Third Parts of King Henry VI, Titus Andronicus, King Richard III, The Comedy of Errors, Love's Labour's Lost, A Midsummer Night's Dream, Romeo and Juliet, King Richard II* (and the long poems *Venus and Adonis* and *The Rape of Lucrece*).

1596–1599  *King John, The Merchant of Venice, First and Second Parts of King Henry IV, The Merry Wives of Windsor, Much Ado About Nothing, King Henry V, Julius Caesar* (and probably the *Sonnets*).

1600–1605  *As You Like It, Hamlet, Twelfth Night, Troilus and Cressida, Measure for Measure, Othello, All's Well That Ends Well, Timon of Athens, King Lear.*

1606–1611  *Macbeth, Antony and Cleopatra, Pericles, Coriolanus, The Winter's Tale, Cymbeline, The Tempest.*

1613  *King Henry VIII, The Two Noble Kinsmen* (both probably with John Fletcher).

1623  Shakespeare's plays published as a collection (now called the First Folio).